THE BOSTON CELTICS

JOHN F. GRABOWSKI

Other Books in the Great Sports Teams Series:

The Chicago Bulls
The Dallas Cowboys
The Los Angeles Dodgers
The Los Angeles Lakers
The Minnesota Vikings
The New York Rangers
The New York Yankees
The San Francisco 49ers

GREAT SPORTS TEAMS

THE BOSTON CELTICS

JOHN F. GRABOWSKI

LUCENT
BOOKS ®

THOMSON

GALE

San Diego • Detroit • New York • San Francisco • Cleveland
New Haven, Conn. • Waterville, Maine • London • Munich

THOMSON

™

GALE

APR − − 2003

LIBRARY OF CONGRESS CATALOGING-IN-PUBLICATION DATA

Grabowski, John F.
    The Boston Celtics / by John F. Grabowski.
    p. cm. — (Great sports teams)
Includes bibliographical references and index.
    ISBN 1-56006-936-8 (hardback : alk. paper)
Contents: Introduction: The Celtics Mystique—The Boston Legacy—Red Auerbach—Bob
Cousy—Bill Russell—John Havlicek—Dave Cowens—Larry Bird.
    1. Boston Celtics (Basketball team)—History—Juvenile literature. [1. Boston Celtics
(Basketball team)—History. 2. Basketball—History. 3. Basketball players.] I. Title. II.
Great sports teams (Lucent Books)
    GV885.52.B67 G716 2003
    796.323'64'0974461—dc21

                                                         2002004892

Printed in the United States of America

Contents

FOREWORD

Former Supreme Court Chief Justice Warren Burger once said he always read the sports section of the newspaper first because it was about humanity's successes, while the front page listed only humanity's failures. Millions of people across the country today would probably agree with Burger's preference for tales of human endurance, record-breaking performances, and feats of athletic prowess. Although these accomplishments are far beyond what most Americans can ever hope to achieve, average people, the fans, do want to affect what happens on the field of play. Thus, their role becomes one of encouragement. They cheer for their favorite players and team and boo the opposition.

ABC Sports president Roone Arledge once attempted to explain the relationship between fan and team. Sport, said Arledge, is "a set of created circumstances—artificial circumstances—set up to frustrate a man in pursuit of a goal. He has to have certain skills to overcome those obstacles—or even to challenge them. And people who don't have those skills cheer him and admire him." Over a period of time, the admirers may develop a rabid—even irrational—allegiance to a particular team. Indeed, the word "fan" itself is derived from the word "fanatic," someone possessed by an excessive and irrational zeal. Sometimes this devotion to a team is because of a favorite player; often it's because of where a person lives, and, occasionally, it's because of a family allegiance to a particular club.

Whatever the reason, the bond formed between team and fan often defies reason. It may be easy to understand the appeal of the New York Yankees, a team that has gone to the World Series an incredible thirty-eight times and won twenty-six championships, nearly three times as many as any other major league baseball team. It is more difficult, though, to comprehend the fanaticism of Chicago Cubs fans, who faithfully follow the progress of a team that hasn't won a World Series since 1908. Regardless, the Cubs have surpassed the 2 million mark in home attendance in fourteen of the last seventeen years. In fact, their two highest totals were posted in 1999 and 2000, when the team finished in last place.

Each volume in Lucent's Great Sports Teams series examines a team that has left its mark on the "American sports consciousness." Each book looks at the history and tradition of the club in an attempt to understand its appeal and the loyalty —even passion—of its fans. Each volume also examines the lives and careers of people who played significant roles in the team's history. Players, managers, coaches, and front-office executives are represented.

Endnoted quotations help bring the text in each book to life. In addition, all books include an annotated bibliography and a For Further Reading list to supply students with sources for conducting additional individual research.

No one volume can hope to explain fully the mystique of the New York Yankees, Boston Celtics, Dallas Cowboys, or Montreal Canadiens. The Lucent Great Sports Teams series, however, gives interested readers a solid start on the road to understanding the mysterious bond that exists between modern professional sports teams and their devoted followers.

The Celtics Mystique

Boston is often referred to as the Hub, short for "hub of the universe." Although some people might consider this somewhat presumptuous, many more consider it true in the world of professional basketball. No team in the history of the sport has matched the success of the Boston Celtics. That success has given rise to a "Celtics mystique" that has been the bane of many a competing team.

Leprechauns and Parquet

Mystique is sometimes defined as an aura of mystery and reverence attached to something believed to possess special power and ability. The Boston Celtics mystique is credited with helping the team win sixteen National Basketball Association (NBA) championships, including eleven over a period of thirteen years. The team always seemed to come up with a basket, rebound, blocked shot, or steal just when it was needed.

Some claimed leprechauns in the rafters of the old Boston Garden were responsible for deflecting opponents' shots away from the basket. Others believed the magic lay in the famous parquet floor, which came into existence as a result of a shortage of long boards during World War II. The floor, it was said, had dead spots in it that were known only to Boston players.

Even the players themselves came to believe some sort of undefined, undescribable force was at work. In an interview for ESPN Classics's *SportsCentury* series, former Celtics forward Paul Silas described his thoughts after being traded to Boston. "When I came to the Celtics," he said, "there was this Celtic mystique. And I was one of the few skeptics. Finally, it came through to me after we had won the championship. I went up to Red and said, 'Now I understand what the Celtic mystique is.' And he was about the proudest man in the world."[1]

Others attributed the mystique to the man Silas

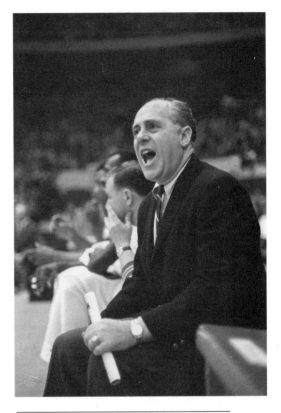

Boston Celtics coach Arnold "Red" Auerbach yells instructions to his players from the sidelines. Auerbach ascribed the mystique of the team to a consistent desire to win.

sought out: coach Red Auerbach. Auerbach convinced the team it could not lose. Opposing clubs came to believe they could not win. Boston Hall of Famer Bob Cousy had perhaps the best explanation of all. When asked what the Celtics' secret was, Cousy replied, "The Celtics' mystique is simply a desire to be first. The players all have the killer instinct. Their desire to win is not diluted by the big money. The Celtic mystique is nothing other than good players who complement each other and all of whom have the killer instinct."[2]

CHAPTER 1

The Boston Legacy

As a charter member of the Basketball Association of America (the forerunner of the National Basketball Association), the Boston Celtics have won more championships than any other team. Many of the greatest players in league history have worn the green and white, including twenty-eight members of the Hall of Fame. The team founded by Walter Brown and built by Red Auerbach has earned a place as one of the greatest dynasties in professional sports.

Birth of a New Pro League

On June 6, 1946, the Boston Celtics franchise came into existence as part of the Basketball Association of America (BAA). The fledgling league was formed by a group of eleven National and American Hockey League arena owners. For the most part, these men, led by Walter Brown of Boston, had no previous experience with basketball. They were mainly interested in reducing their overhead by filling their arenas on days when hockey was not on the schedule. With college basketball enjoying a surge in popularity, the time seemed right to gamble on the new enterprise.

The Boston franchise was operated by Brown, whose father had been general manager of the Boston Arena. The son had been involved in sports for most of his life. He founded the Boston Olympics amateur hockey club and later coached the 1936 United States Olympic hockey team to a bronze medal in the 1936 Berlin Summer Olympics. When his father died in 1937, Walter replaced him as general manager of the Garden-Arena Corporation. (By this time, the corporation operated both Boston Arena and the newer Boston Garden.) He would have a profound effect on the future of pro basketball.

Looking for a local name to attract fans to the games, Brown wanted Rhode Island University coach Frank Keaney to lead his new team. After accepting the offer, Keaney backed out at the last minute because of health problems. Brown then turned to former Seton Hall coaching legend John "Honey" Russell, who was hired for the position.

The Celtics played their first home game on November 5, 1946. The start of the contest was held up for an hour when Boston's Chuck Connors (the future star of television's *The Rifleman)* splintered a wooden backboard with a dunk during pregame practice. After the damage was repaired, the crowd of 4,329 fans settled down to see the team lose to the Chicago Stags, 57-55.

With center Connie Simmons as its best player, Boston struggled to a 22-38 record in the league's inaugural season of 1946–47. The Celtics won only twenty games the next year but managed to make the postseason playoffs, where they lost to the Chicago Stags.

The team continued to struggle in 1948–49, both on the court under new coach Alvin "Doggie" Julian and at the box office. When unhappy stockholders wanted to sell their shares, Brown bought them out. He eventually remortgaged his home to keep the club going. The next year the league solidified itself by absorbing six teams from the National Basketball League (NBL) and changing its name to the National Basketball Association.

The Arrival of Red Auerbach

The Celtics made news in 1950 when they signed former Tri-Cities Blackhawks coach Red Auerbach to replace Julian. Owner Walter Brown continued to handle business operations,

Red Auerbach poses for the camera in his third year as head coach of the Boston Celtics.

but unoffically gave all control of basketball operations, including scouting, coaching, and general management to Auerbach. Red took the responsibility and ran with it.

When the St. Louis Bombers franchise folded, Boston obtained promising center "Easy Ed" Macauley in a dispersal draft in the league's attempt to strengthen its weaker teams. Macauley would become the first Celtics player to average twenty points a game over the course of a season.

Of even more historical significance was a move Auerbach made in the 1950 college draft. With the team's second pick, he selected forward Chuck Cooper of Duquesne, the first black player drafted by an NBA team. Auerbach would later become the first NBA coach to start five black players and the first person to hire a black coach (Bill Russell).

Soon after, a major piece of good fortune came Boston's way. Just before the season was scheduled to begin, the Chicago Stags went out of business. Once again the remaining teams scrambled for the available players. The New York Knicks, Philadelphia Warriors, and Celtics were allowed to choose one of three guards—veterans Max Zaslofsky and Andy Phillip and rookie Bob Cousy. When none of the clubs agreed to take Cousy, they decided to put the players' names in a hat. New York selected first and picked Zaslofsky. Philadelphia chose next and got Phillip. The Celtics were left with the rookie. Cousy would prove to be an immediate hit and develop into one of the NBA's all-time greats.

Auerbach's new players immediately produced results. The team employed a fastbreaking style that helped lead it to its first winning record in the franchise's history (39-30). The year ended on a negative note when the Celtics were upset by the Knicks in the playoffs, but the team at last seemed to be headed in a positive direction.

Building a Contender

The next season (1951–52) another important piece was added to the puzzle. Sharp-shooting guard Bill Sharman was obtained in a trade with the Fort Wayne Pistons. He teamed with Cousy to form one of the league's all-time great backcourt combinations.

Bob Cousy (left) poses with Bill Sharman (right). The pair formed a seemingly invincible backcourt combination in the early 1950s.

Boston took another step forward in 1952–53 when the team won a postseason series for the first time. The Celtics defeated the Syracuse Nationals in the Eastern Division Semifinals before losing to the New York Knickerbockers in the division finals. They advanced to the division finals again in each of the next two seasons but lost to Syracuse both times. When the league adopted the twenty-four-second clock in 1954–55, the high-powered Celtics became the first NBA team to average one hundred points a game for a season. Unfortunately, because of their porous defense, they also were the first club to allow one hundred points a game. Auerbach realized the team needed a defensive presence if it was to advance to the next level. He was to find that presence in the 1956 draft.

A Thrilling Finish

The 1956 draft proved to be a bonanza for the Celtics. First, the team claimed Holy Cross University forward Tom Heinsohn as a territorial pick. (At the time, NBA rules allowed this special draft for players who had played college ball in a team's geographical region, to please local fans and sell more tickets.) The rugged Heinsohn would go on to average 18.6 points per game over his nine-year career and play in six All-Star games. Guard K.C. Jones was another smart selection. Following a two-year stint in the army, the University of San Francisco defensive whiz joined the team in 1958 and played nine seasons in the NBA. Both Heinsohn and Jones would win championships coaching the Celtics and be elected to the Naismith Memorial Basketball Hall of Fame.

The biggest prize of all, however, was center Bill Russell, also from San Francisco. Russell would revolutionize the game of basketball with his defense. In the process, he transformed the Celtics from a contending team into the most dominant club in the history of professional sports.

With Russell keying the vaunted Celtics fast break with his shot-blocking, rebounding, and quick outlet passes, Boston raced to the best record in the league. The Celtics swept Syracuse in the three-game Eastern Division Finals series, then defeated the St. Louis Hawks in an exciting seven-game set for their first NBA championship.

Celtics center Bill Russell hooks a shot over a St. Louis Hawks defender. Russell was a key factor in the Celtics' first NBA championship in 1957.

The deciding contest was one of the most memorable games in the history of the league. A national television audience watched the game, which helped solidify the status of professional basketball as a national sport. The Hawks and Celtics battled back and forth for forty-eight minutes with neither team able to pull away. St. Louis forward Bob Pettit sank two free throws in the final seconds to send the game into overtime. In the final seconds of the five-minute extra period, the Hawks scored to force a second overtime. Down by two points with time running out in the second extra stanza, the Hawks tried an unorthodox play in an attempt to tie the score once again. St. Louis player-coach Alex Hannum put the ball in play by heaving it the length of the court off the Boston backboard. The ball bounced into Pettit's hands, but his last-second shot ricocheted off the rim to give Boston the win.

The title was truly a team affair, something that was to become a Celtics trademark. Russell averaged nearly twenty rebounds per game, Cousy led the NBA in assists and was named the league's Most Valuable Player, Heinsohn won Rookie of the Year honors, and Bill Sharman was the team's leading scorer. Six players averaged double figures in points scored including Frank Ramsey, who would build a reputation as the league's best "sixth man."

The Making of a Dynasty

The Hawks gained a measure of revenge in the 1957–58 season. For the second year in a row, the Celtics compiled the best record in the league. In the playoffs they once again met the Hawks in the finals. Russell was injured in Game 3 and could not perform at full strength. The Hawks took advantage and dethroned the Celtics in six games. Bob Pettit's fifty points paced St. Louis in the 110-109 clincher.

With the defeat at the hands of the Hawks still fresh in their minds, the 1958–59 Celtics began the season intent on regaining their championship crown. Not only did they accomplish their goal, they went on to attain a level of success never before achieved by any professional sports franchise. The Celtics would put together an incredible streak of eight consecutive championships before having their run ended in 1967.

The 1958–59 squad was strengthened by the addition of guard K.C. Jones following his army service. Boston dominated the NBA, leading the league in points scored, rebounds, and assists while surpassing fifty wins for the first time in franchise history. (They would do so in each of the next nine seasons.) On February 27 the team scored 173 points in a victory over the Minneapolis Lakers to set a single-game record that would stand for twenty-four years. That April, those same Lakers would be swept in a four-game series to give the Celtics the title.

Championship number two came in a year marked by a record-tying seventeen-game winning streak. The 1959–60 season also saw the beginning of professional basketball's most famous individual rivalry. Seven-foot, one-inch rookie Wilt Chamberlain exploded on the pro scene with the Philadelphia Warriors and led the league in scoring. His numerous battles with Bill Russell would dominate NBA headlines for years to come. Chamberlain often came out on top statistically, but Russell's Celtics were victorious more often than not. In the first of their playoff matchups, the Celtics defeated the Warriors in the six-game Eastern Division Finals. They then disposed of the Hawks in seven games to win the crown.

Forward Tom Sanders joined the Celtics in 1960, and the team rolled to fifty-seven wins. In their easiest playoff run of all, they routed Syracuse and St.

Philadelphia center, Wilt Chamberlain, goes head to head with Bill Russell (right). Battles between the two were an exciting feature of NBA action throughout the late 1950s and 1960s.

Louis, losing only two of ten contests. In doing so, they became the second team in league history to win three consecutive championships. (The Minneapolis Lakers of 1952–54 were the first.)

The 1961–62 NBA season was marked by several noteworthy performances. Wilt Chamberlain set an all-time record by averaging 50.4 points per game. Cincinnati's Oscar Robertson performed an equally impressive feat by averaging a triple-double (double digits in three categories: 30.8 points, 12.5 rebounds, and 11.4 assists) for the entire season. Despite these notable individual achievements, the Celtics still dominated as a team, becoming the first NBA club to win sixty games in a season on their way to their fourth title in a row.

At the beginning of the 1962–63 season, Bob Cousy announced it would be his last. The Celtics had another superstar waiting in the wings, however, having selected John Havlicek of Ohio State in the college draft. Boston won fifty-eight games, then defeated the Cincinnati Royals and the Lakers in the playoffs to give Cousy one final championship ring. The following year sixth-man Havlicek led the team in scoring, coming off the bench as the Celtics won their sixth crown in a row.

Shortly before the 1964–65 season began, Celtics founder Walter Brown died at age sixty-four, and the team dedicated the season to the beloved Boston owner. In a ceremony on October 17, uniform number 1 was retired in his honor. As coach, and now officially general manager, Red Auerbach declared, "He personified everything good in sports."[3]

The Celtics proceeded to win sixty-two games to set another new franchise mark. Their march to the title was nearly short-circuited by the Philadelphia 76ers in the Eastern Division Finals. In one of the great moments in Celtics history, however, John Havlicek stole an inbound pass with seconds to go in Game 7 to seal the victory. The club then trounced the Los Angeles Lakers in the NBA Finals for its seventh consecutive championship.

That June the Celtics were purchased by Ruppert-Knickerbocker Breweries and National Equities. The change in ownership did not hamper the club's run toward another title in 1965–66. Neither did the midyear announcement of Red Auerbach's retirement as coach at the end of the season. Boston failed to win the Eastern Division crown after a ten-year run at the top as the 76ers edged them out by one game. In the playoffs, however, the Celtics magic still held. After a hard-fought five-game Eastern Division Semifinals series win over the Royals, Boston breezed past Philadelphia in the division finals.

The NBA Finals matched the Celtics against the Lakers. After Boston lost Game 1, Auerbach announced that Bill Russell would succeed him as coach of the team. The Celtics responded by taking four of the next six games to win the title—their amazing eighth straight NBA championship.

A Change in Command

In addition to taking over as head coach, Russell remained active as a player, and the Celtics continued to be one of the league's top teams. In 1966–67, the club actually improved its record in the regular season, winning six more games than it did in Auerbach's final year. The 76ers, however, displaced them from the top spot in the Eastern Division. Philadelphia compiled an amazing 68-13 record, finishing eight games ahead of Boston. The team many called the greatest in NBA history defeated the Celtics in the Eastern Division Finals to end Boston's championship streak. With several Celtics players nearing retirement age, it appeared to many that the dynasty was at an end. The Celtics, however, proved otherwise.

Boston finished eight games behind Philadelphia in 1967–68 and again faced the 76ers in the playoffs. This time the under-dog Celtics prevailed. They defeated the 76ers in an exciting seven-game series, then bested the Los Angeles Lakers in the NBA Finals to give Russell his first ring as head coach.

The Celtics followed a similar path in 1968–69. This time they finished fourth in the Eastern Division with forty-eight wins, their lowest regular-season total since the 1956–57 season. In the playoffs they rose to the occasion, first beating Philadelphia then New York to reach the finals. The Lakers of Wilt Chamberlain, Jerry West, and Elgin Baylor were their opponents. After losing the first two games to Los Angeles, the Celtics bounced back. Tied at three games apiece, Boston built an early lead in Game 7, and then they held on to win for the team's eleventh championship in thirteen years. Russell stepped down—as Auerbach had—on a winning note.

John Havlicek shoots a running hook over the arms of a Milwaukee Bucks defender in a 1974 NBA playoff game.

The End of One Era
and the Start of Another

Tom Heinsohn was named by Auerbach as the team's new coach. The loss of Russell on the court, however, was impossible to overcome. Boston finished with a record below .500—and out of the playoffs—for the first time in twenty years. Rookie center Dave Cowens joined the team in 1970 and helped the Celtics improve to 44-38. It was not enough to put them in the playoffs, however. The high point of the NBA's twenty-fifth season came when the Silver Anniversary Team was announced. Celtic representatives on the squad were Red Auerbach (who was named team president as well as general manager in 1970), Bob Cousy, Bill Russell, Bill Sharman, and Sam Jones.

With Cowens and Havlicek anchoring the team, Boston was soon back on top. They finished in first place in the Atlantic Division (created in 1970 when the league was reorganized) in each of the next five seasons. In 1972–73 they set the franchise's all-time single-season record with sixty-eight wins against only fourteen defeats.

Boston won its next championship in 1973–74. In one of the most exciting NBA Finals, the Celtics defeated Kareem Abdul-Jabbar and the Milwaukee Bucks in seven thrilling games. Two years later they repeated as champs by beating the Phoenix Suns in the finals. Game 5 of that series is considered one of the greatest playoff contests of all time. Phoenix's Paul Westphal scored five points in the final minute of regulation time to help the Suns tie the score. The first overtime also ended in a tie. In the second extra period a last-second basket by Phoenix's Garfield Heard knotted the score once again. The Celtics finally eked out a 128-126 win in three overtimes, making the game the longest in NBA Finals history. An 87-80 win in Game 6 gave Boston its thirteenth NBA championship.

After five years at the top of the Atlantic Division, Boston fell to second place in 1976–77. When the club got off to a slow start the next season (on the way to a fifth-place finish), Heinsohn was fired and replaced by Tom Sanders. It would not be long, however, before the team returned to the league's upper echelon.

The Greatest Ballplayer Ever

The summer of 1978 was a prominent one in Celtics history. On June 9, 1978, the team drafted forward Larry Bird of Indiana State University. The move by Red Auerbach was an unusual one since Bird still had one season of college eligibility left. Less than a month later the Celtics and Buffalo Braves swapped owners, with former Kentucky governor John Y. Brown taking over as head man. When the season opened, the team lost twelve of its first fourteen games. It finished with a disappointing record of 29-53, stuck in last place in the division.

Bill Fitch was hired as head coach following the end of the season. Led by rookie sensation Bird, the Celtics returned to the top of the Atlantic Division. The team's thirty-two-game improvement over the previous year helped earn Fitch Coach of the Year honors.

A trade with the Golden State Warriors in June 1980 provided the final pieces of the puzzle. In the deal, Boston obtained

Larry Bird proudly displays his Celtics jersey at a 1978 news conference after being signed by the team.

center Robert Parish together with a draft choice that would turn out to be rugged forward Kevin McHale. The front line of Parish, McHale, and Bird helped the team overcome the loss of center Dave Cowens, who retired during training camp. Boston compiled a 62-20 record on the way to yet another championship.

Bird, the man whom Auerbach would later call "the greatest ballplayer who ever played the game,"[4] led the Celtics to two more titles (1983–84 and 1985–86) and two other appearances in the NBA Finals (1984–85 and 1986–87). The team won at least fifty games in all but one of his thirteen seasons and surpassed sixty on six occasions. In ten of those years, the Celtics finished in first place in the Atlantic Division during the regular season.

A Pair of Tragedies

The 1985–86 season was perhaps Bird's greatest. In leading Boston to sixty-seven wins, Bird finished fourth in the league in scoring, seventh in rebounds, and ninth in steals. He also led the NBA in free throw percentage and finished fourth in three-point field goal percentage. Bird won his third consecutive Most Valuable Player trophy as Boston dominated in the play-offs, winning fifteen of eighteen games to earn its sixteenth NBA crown.

Despite having won the title, the Celtics were an aging team. In an effort to bring new life to the club Auerbach drafted University of Maryland star Len Bias with the second pick of the 1986 draft, envisioning him as the perfect partner at forward for Larry Bird. Unfortunately, it was not meant to be. Two days after being selected Bias died of a drug overdose.

The Celtics overcame the tragic loss to win their fourth consecutive Atlantic Division title under coach K.C. Jones. They followed with a fifth in 1987–88, but the team faltered in the playoffs both years. The big three of Bird, Parish, and McHale helped keep the team in contention over the next four years, but aside from guard Reggie Lewis, prospects for the future did not look bright.

Bird retired prior to the 1992–93 season, but the Celtics still managed to reach the playoffs. They made a quick exit in their first round series with the Charlotte Hornets, however, a series marked by Lewis's collapse on the court in Game 1. He was later diagnosed with an irregular heartbeat. Sadly, tragedy struck again later that summer. While shooting baskets one day, Lewis again collapsed and went into cardiac arrest. He died soon after.

The Long Struggle Back

The years following Lewis's death were the bleakest period in Celtics history. Beginning with 1993–94, the club put together a streak of eight consecutive losing seasons, reaching the play-offs only in 1994–95. Even hiring a new coach (M.L. Carr) and christening a new home court (Fleet Center) could not stem the tide. The low point came in 1996–97 when the team compiled a

An animated Celtics head coach, Rick Pitino, motions from the sidelines during a recent game. Pitino struggled to put the team back on top.

franchise-worst 15-67 mark and finished in last place in the Atlantic Division, forty-six games out of first.

Before the beginning of the 1997–98 season, Red Auerbach was promoted to the position of vice-chairman of the Celtics board. Rick Pitino, who led the University of Kentucky to the NCAA championship two years before, was hired as head coach and team president. Taking over the day-to-day operations of the club, Pitino looked forward to the task of returning Boston to its former dominance.

Such was not to be the case, however. The Celtics improved by twenty-one games their first season under Pitino but failed to progress further. On January 8, 2001, he resigned after three and a half seasons in charge. Pitino's team never finished better than ten games below .500 as he compiled a cumulative record of 102 wins and 146 losses. Assistant coach Jim O'Brien took over the team fully realizing the position he was in. "The Boston Celtics," he said, "is a franchise I am proud to be a part of, the championship tradition is something that I have actually been in awe of and I understand the need to get back into the playoffs and further."[5] Under O'Brien, the Celtics began to show new life. The team finished strong in 2000–01 and got off to a fast start the next season.

With basketball talent divided among more than twice as many teams in the NBA today than existed in the 1960s, it is unlikely any modern-day club will ever duplicate Boston's feat of winning eight consecutive league championships. "I will wager two months of my life that that record will never be surpassed," says Bob Cousy. "It took another 20 years before another NBA team even won back-to-back titles."[6] Fifteen years have gone by since the team's last title, and Celtics fans are understandably anxious for another winner. With hopes for the future resting on players such as former first-round picks Antoine Walker and Paul Pierce, the Celtics hope to build on their recent improvement and return soon to the league's upper level.

CHAPTER 2

Red Auerbach

R ed Auerbach is the most successful coach in the history of the NBA. His eight straight championships—and eleven in thirteen years—is a record that likely will never be matched. The irascible Auerbach was despised by many for his relentless drive to win at all costs, but no one can argue with the results. He was the master architect behind one of sport's all-time great dynasties.

The Kid from Brooklyn

Arnold Jacob Auerbach, the second child of Hyman and Marie Auerbach, was born on September 20, 1917, in the Williamsburg section of Brooklyn, New York. His father was a Russian Jew who came to America when he was just thirteen years old. He married his American-born wife and set about making a life for his family. At various times, he owned a small restaurant, a delicatessen, and a dry-cleaning business.

The Auerbachs had four children: Victor preceded Arnold, who was followed by Zangwell and Florence. Arnold, whom everyone called Red because of his auburn hair, was the athlete of the family. As Victor recalled, "He was a good, good athlete, and he was also very bright. . . . But he never studied as hard as he should

26

have because he was too interested in playing ball."[7]

Red was introduced to basketball at P.S. 122. "In my area of Brooklyn," he explains, "there was no football, no baseball. They were too expensive. They didn't have the practice fields. We played basketball and handball and some softball in the street."[8] By the time he entered Eastern District High School, Red was good enough to make the varsity team as a guard. Small but very competitive, in his senior year he captained the squad and was named to the All-Brooklyn Second Team. At the same time, he was captain of the handball team and president of the student body.

Coach Red Auerbach watches the clock run out, his trademark victory cigar in plain view.

Red's career goal was to become a teacher and coach. Upon his graduation in 1936, he entered Seth Low Junior College, a branch of Columbia University, on an athletic scholarship. The school closed after his freshman year, and he accepted a scholarship to George Washington University, where he played three seasons for coach Bill Reinhart. In his senior year Auerbach was the Colonials captain and high scorer. As former teammate Bob Faris recalls, "Reinhart was the domineering factor, of course, but it was Red who more or less set up our whole offense and made it go. He had quite a head on his shoulders."[9]

Auerbach was a student of the game. Under Reinhart he learned the value of the fast break. It was a maneuver that would become an essential component of his future Celtics strategy.

Following his graduation with a degree in physical education, Auerbach remained at George Washington. He earned his master's degree with a thesis on physical education programs at the junior high school level. At the same time he worked at a variety of jobs to gain experience in the fields of coaching and teaching.

The Pros Beckon

With his master's in hand, Auerbach accepted a position at Roosevelt High School in Washington in 1941. In addition to teaching history and hygiene, he also coached the school's basketball and baseball teams. Two years later, in mid-World War II, he enlisted in the navy. At the Norfolk Naval Station Auerbach was involved in the physical education program, organizing intramural tournaments and coaching basketball. Included among his players were several of the top former college stars of the day.

Bill Reinhart (pictured) was Auerbach's basketball coach at George Washington University.

Shortly after Red was discharged he heard about the formation of a new professional basketball league. One of the Basketball Association of America franchises was earmarked for Washington, and Auerbach jumped at the opportunity to continue his involvement in the sport he loved. Auerbach applied for the job of head coach and was hired by owner Mike Uline.

Auerbach had a definite plan in mind. He wanted specific players he had known in the navy and went about procuring their services. His plan worked to perfection. The Washington Capitols became the dominant team in the Eastern Division of the new league. They ran off a seventeen-game winning streak early in the 1946–47 season and finished the year in first place with a record of 49-11. Unfortunately, the Caps were eliminated by the Western Division-champion Chicago Stags in the first round of the postseason playoffs. Auerbach, however, impressed many people with his coaching abilities. As former Philadelphia Warriors coach Eddie Gottlieb notes, "Even at that young age [twenty-nine], Red showed he knew how to spot talent, and then get the very most out of it."[10]

In two more years with Washington Auerbach's teams finished third and first in their division. In 1949 they advanced to the final round of the playoffs, where they lost to George Mikan and the powerful Minneapolis Lakers. In Auerbach's three seasons at the helm the Caps compiled a record of 115-53 for a winning percentage of .685. It was the best mark, by far, of any of the league's coaches.

Although Auerbach achieved great success, he did so in a way that bothered many people. As former NBA commissioner Walter Kennedy remembers, "He had the qualities of brashness, cockiness and confidence way back then, and because of that— and also because of the great success his team enjoyed—there seemed to be a great resentment towards the Caps. . . . He could raise an awful commotion."[11]

After the 1948–49 season, Auerbach quit the Caps following a contract dispute. He accepted a job as an advisory coach and assistant professor at Duke University. Before long, however, he was back in the pros as coach of the Tri-Cities Blackhawks. He lasted just one year in the position, quitting when owner Ben Kerner made a trade against his wishes. As Auerbach later explained, "I quit telling him if he had no confidence in my judgment of talent I was worthless to him."[12] The thirty-two-year-old Auerbach was again out of a job, but not for long. He was soon contacted by Boston Celtics owner Walter Brown and offered a position as the team's coach.

Evolution of the Celtic Mystique

The four-year-old Celtics club had not yet had a winning season. After finishing in last place in the Eastern Division in 1949–50, the team seemed on the brink of financial disaster. This was the situation Auerbach faced when he accepted Brown's offer.

Celtics guard Bob Cousy takes a pass during practice. Cousy was pivotal in the early success of the team.

Auerbach immediately went to work putting his mark on the team. With his first pick in the 1950 college draft, he selected six-foot, eleven-inch center Chuck Share from Bowling Green University. It was an unpopular move with the fans, who had been expecting Boston to take electrifying playmaker Bob Cousy from nearby Holy Cross. (Failing to draft Cousy would prove to be one of Auerbach's few errors in judging talent.)

Over the next few months Auerbach completely rebuilt the Celtics, with luck playing a significant role in the process. Six of the league's teams folded before the season began, and the Celtics were able to obtain Cousy and six-foot, nine-inch center Ed Macauley when players from those clubs became available. By the time the 1950–51 season opened with a reorganized league renamed the National Basketball Association (NBA), only two players remained from the previous year's team.

Boston began the year by losing its first three games and then proceeded to win seven in a row. The team never fell below the .500 mark and finished the year with a record of 39-30—the fourth-best mark in the ten-team league. The Celtics lost to the Knicks in the playoffs, but no one could deny their improvement. Auerbach had taken a club headed for disaster and transformed it into an exciting, winning basketball team.

Over the next five seasons the Celtics continued to be an above-average team, never finishing with a record below .500. Sharpshooting guard Bill Sharman and brawny forward Bob Brannum joined the club in 1951–52, but the team still struggled in the playoffs. Its fast-break offense put points on the scoreboard, but its defense was one of the worst in the league. As Auerbach told one sportswriter following the Celtics' exit from the playoffs after the 1955–56 season, "With the talent we've got on this team, if we can just come up with one big man to get us the ball, we'll win everything in sight."[13] It would not be long before Auerbach found his big man.

The Trade

The Celtics owned the third pick in the 1956 college draft. Auerbach desperately wanted to select defensive wizard Bill Russell from the University of San Francisco. He could not be sure, however, that the six-foot, nine-inch Russell would not be taken by the St. Louis Hawks, who drafted second. (The Rochester Royals, who had the number one pick, could not afford the salary Russell would demand.) To guarantee that he would get his man, Auerbach traded Macauley and rookie Cliff Hagan to St. Louis in exchange for the draft rights to Russell. In doing so he forever changed the face of the National Basketball Association.

Russell proved to be an immediate sensation. He joined the Celtics after leading the U.S. Olympic basketball team to a gold medal in the 1956 Summer Games in Melbourne, Australia. Russell became the cornerstone of the Boston defense with his shot-blocking, rebounding, and quick outlet passes. The Celtics raced to a 44-28 record in the regular season to finish first in the

Bill Russell (right) signs a contract with Celtics representatives. Russell quickly established himself as the heart of the team's defense.

Eastern Division. They then defeated the Syracuse Nationals and St. Louis Hawks in the playoffs to win their first NBA championship.

Game 3 of the finals series against the Hawks was marked by an ugly incident that wound up costing Auerbach $300. Prior to the contest in St. Louis, Auerbach insisted that the referees check the height of the Celtics basket, thinking it might have been altered to give the Hawks an advantage. Hawks owner Ben Kerner, Auerbach's former boss in his year with the Tri-Cities Blackhawks, was infuriated, thinking Auerbach was trying to intimidate the referees and rouse his team. "You're really bush!" yelled Kerner at his former coach.[14] Auerbach charged Kerner and threw a punch that drew blood from his lip. After reviewing the incident, NBA commissioner Maurice Podoloff announced that Auerbach would be fined.

The following season the Celtics again finished first in the East. They were defeated by the Hawks in the NBA Finals, however, when Russell injured his ankle. In 1958–59 they won their second title to begin an incredible streak of eight consecutive league championships. No other team in any professional sport has ever duplicated that feat.

The Auerbach Style

Auerbach's strategy in building a team was to find players who put the team before themselves. According to forward Tom Heinsohn, "He had a touch with people and could get them committed to what he was doing. He made the Celtics into basketball's Cosa Nostra. We believed it was our thing."[15]

Although the Celtics had great shooters, no player on Auerbach's teams led the league in scoring. His players' talents and styles complemented each other, and the result was a club that was much more than the sum of its parts. Boston popularized the concept of the "role player." According to Auerbach, "That's a player who willingly undertakes the thankless job that has to be done in order to make the whole package fly."[16]

Auerbach also believed in the idea of having a strong sixth man, or first player off the bench. Frank Ramsey—and later John Havlicek—was perfect in this role. When the other team's starters began to get tired, a fresh Ramsey or Havlicek came in to provide the Celtics with a burst of energy. The result was often a completely demoralized opponent. As sportswriter Jim Murray wrote in a 1963 column, "They play a different game from anyone else in the sport. It's more of a track meet than basketball. They have so many so good that Auerbach keeps shuttling them in until the opposition begins to feel like General Custer."[17]

Coach Auerbach drafted number 23, Frank Ramsey, to be his sixth man, or first player off the bench.

Auerbach was a strict disciplinarian who insisted on complete control of the team. He had the last word as far as trades, salaries, and playing time was concerned. "It was Red's show," says forward Tom Sanders. "[Owner] Walter Brown gave him complete control."[18]

Auerbach had a fierce determination to win and was able to instill a killer instinct in his players. He motivated them by appealing to their pride. When they returned to camp after a summer off, he asked them, "Did you have a good summer? How did it feel to be a member of the greatest basketball team in the world? Now, do you want to give that away?"[19] Under his constant prodding the Celtics eventually acted and played as though they expected to win. That air of invincibility was a key component of the Celtic mystique.

The Victory Cigar

Auerbach and his players expected to win every time they set foot on the court. When the coach thought victory was certain, he would light up a cigar on the bench. This victory cigar was increasingly galling to opposing players, coaches, and fans. Even his own players disliked the habit. "It made us all uncomfortable," explains Bob Cousy. "When he did this, it got everyone's attention. . . . He sat benignly and comfortably on the bench, smoking away, with a guard behind him. Meanwhile, we were out on the floor taking all this abuse. . . . The fans would get more belligerent and hostile toward us, and we had to bust our tails to keep the lead because once he went for the cigar, the other team's intensity went up 100 percent."[20]

According to Auerbach, however, any arrogance was completely unintended. "To me," he explains, "the game was over. . . . So I would light a cigar and sit on the bench and just watch it. . . . I didn't want to rub anything in or show anybody what a great coach I was when I was 25 points ahead. Why? I gotta win by 30?"[21]

Into the Front Office

No matter how intense the pressure, Auerbach's teams rarely lost. By the time he retired at age forty-eight following the 1965–66 season, he was the winningest coach in NBA history with 938 victories and only 479 defeats. His nine NBA championships have only been matched by Phil Jackson.

Auerbach named Bill Russell as his successor and moved into the Celtics front office as general manager. He remained in that position through 1984, by which time he had added six more championship rings. As general manager (and team president, beginning in 1970), Auerbach put together his championship teams through a combination of shrewd trades and a keen evaluation of young talent. Perhaps his best deal was with the San Francisco Warriors in 1980. The Celtics received center Robert Parish and a draft pick that would turn out to be forward Kevin

Auerbach lights another victory cigar. By several measures, Auerbach is the most successful coach in NBA history.

McHale. In exchange, Boston sent San Francisco the number one pick in the draft, which the Warriors used to select the underachieving seven-foot center Joe Barry Carroll.

Auerbach's crowning achievement was selecting future Hall of Famer Larry Bird in the 1978 draft. Other teams bypassed Bird, who was just a junior, knowing he would not play until another college season had passed. (He was eligible for the draft since his senior class had graduated a month earlier.) "They didn't know he'd be that good," says Auerbach, "and I didn't either. I only saw him play once."[22] When he eventually joined the Celtics, he proved to be well worth the wait.

After stepping down as general manager Auerbach remained team president, winning a sixteenth title in that capacity in 1985–86. He held that position until 1997, when he was promoted to vice-chairman of the board. New coach Rick Pitino took over the duties of president. When Pitino resigned in 2001, Auerbach once again added the title of president to his vice-chairman title.

In addition to his work with the Celtics, Auerbach also devotes time to the Red Auerbach Youth Foundation. The foundation raises money to help bring children from all backgrounds together through sports programs. One of the events staged by the foundation is the Red Auerbach Youth Foundation Celebrity Golf Tournament, in which former Boston players often take part. As John Havlicek explains, "Red is the lifeblood of the Boston Celtics, the godfather, the man who created everything there is about the Boston Celtics, he has done so much for so many people that they want to pay back any way they can. This is obviously one of the ways we can do it."[23]

Few have approached Auerbach's record as a coach. When he stepped down in 1966 he had more wins (938) than any coach in league history. Although his total has since been surpassed by Lenny Wilkens, Pat Riley, Don Nelson, and Bill Fitch, Riley is the only one of the four with a higher winning percentage than Auerbach. In addition, it is almost certain that no one will ever match his incredible record of eight consecutive NBA championships.

Auerbach's name will always be synonymous with the Celtics and with winning. As Celtics chairman of the board Paul Gaston said in 2001, "Red Auerbach has been the cornerstone of our franchise for over the past five decades and he was the man who developed the tradition of the Boston Celtics."[24]

CHAPTER 3

Bob Cousy

Known as the Houdini of the Hardwoods, Bob Cousy was basketball's first ballhandling wizard. His behind-the-back dribbles and blind passes led the Celtics' famous fast-break attack and earned him eight NBA assist titles. He was also a productive scorer whose fierce intensity on the court helped lead the Celtics to six league championships.

The East Side of Town

The man who came to be known throughout the sports world simply as "the Cooz" was born Robert Joseph Cousy in a run-down tenement in the Yorkville section of New York City on August 9, 1928. His parents, Joseph and Juliet, had arrived in this country from France less than a year before his birth. His father, who drove a cab, was a native of Alsace-Lorraine. His mother was born in New York but moved to France with her family when she was just four.

French was the language of the Cousy household. Young Roby did not speak English until the age of five and retained a French accent thereafter. His friends began calling him Frenchy. (This later became Flenchy when they noticed he pronounced his *r*'s as *l*'s.)

Bob Cousy demonstrates his shooting prowess honed at the College of the Holy Cross.

As a child living on New York's East Side, Roby played all the games popular with the city kids of the day, but his favorite was stickball. It was not until the family moved to St. Albans, Queens, when he was eleven that the boy became acquainted with basketball. It was love at first sight. The sport quickly became Roby's obsession. As a neighbor told Stanley Frank for a 1954 article in the *Saturday Evening Post*, "He never even went to the movies. I never saw a person as crazy about anything as he was about basketball."[25]

With the help of a local playground director named Morty Arkin, Bob learned the fundamentals of the game. Arkin taught him the correct way to shoot and encouraged him in every way he could. The results quickly became evident. Bob made the junior varsity basketball team at Andrew Jackson High School as a sophomore in 1943, then advanced to the varsity the next year.

Bob couldn't play until February, however, because of a failing grade he received in his citizenship class. When he finally did get into a game, he made the most of his chance. He scored twenty-eight points for coach Lew Grummond's squad against Bryant High, a total that at the time was close to the school record. Bob continued his solid play for the remainder of his junior year. He led Andrew Jackson to the city championships where they advanced to the semifinals before being eliminated. By the end of the season Cousy was being touted as one of the top players in the city.

Bob was named cocaptain in his senior year at Jackson. He led the team to a second consecutive Queens Division title, but the club again was eliminated in the city championships, this time in the quarterfinals. Cousy won the Public Schools Athletic League (PSAL) scoring title and capped his season by being named captain of the city all-scholastic team. The caption next to his picture in the 1946 Jackson school yearbook predicted great things for him. It read: "Bob Cousy, who plays a mighty fine game / Will be among those of basketball fame."[26] Soon afterward, Bob accepted a scholarship offer from the College of the Holy Cross in Worcester, Massachusetts. He would be playing ball there for coach Alvin "Doggie" Julian.

An All-American Career

Cousy entered Holy Cross as a six-foot-tall freshman guard in the fall of 1946. Julian put together a powerful team that finished the year with a record of 27-3. The team made it to the postseason National Collegiate Athletic Association (NCAA) tournament, where they dazzled everyone by winning the national title.

Despite the team's success, however, Cousy was unhappy. He was not playing as much as he had hoped he would and seriously considered transferring to St. John's University in New York. He wrote to St. John's basketball coach, Joe Lapchick, asking for his help. Lapchick's reply made him reconsider his decision. "You're not in college primarily to play basketball," wrote Lapchick, "but to get an education, and you're getting a very good one at Holy Cross. . . . Doggie Julian is one of the finest basketball coaches in America, and some day you'll be proud you've played for him. . . . I know he is depending heavily on you in future years and would be very much upset if he knew how you felt."[27]

Cousy decided to stay at Holy Cross and proceeded to help the team reach the NCAA tournament once again. The Crusaders lost to Kentucky in the second round, however, and were thwarted in their bid to repeat as champions. After the season, Julian left the school to become head coach of the Boston Celtics. He was succeeded by Lester "Buster" Sheary.

The Cooz enjoyed two excellent seasons playing for Sheary. He averaged 17.8 points per game as a junior and then raised his mark to 19.4 as a senior while winning All-American honors in 1949–50. In addition to his scoring Cousy gained fame as an electrifying ball handler, throwing no-look passes to his teammates and occasionally dribbling the ball behind his back.

The first time he tried such a move was in a game against Loyola of Chicago in his junior year. With just ten seconds left to play and needing a basket to win, Cousy drove toward the hoop and found his way blocked by a Loyola player. In his autobiography, *Basketball Is My Life,* Cousy explains what happened next: "There was only one thing left: to shift hands behind my back if I could. I'd never tried it, but I had no choice. So without changing direction, I bounced the ball behind my back with my right hand and picked it up with my left, then drove in and dunked the winning basket into the hoop with a left-handed hook shot. The whole place went nuts and so did I."[28] Such flashy moves drew roars from the fans and helped earn him a reputation as a crowd pleaser.

An Unwanted Rookie

Despite Cousy's success in college, many pro teams questioned his ability to play in the NBA because of his relatively short height (six feet, one inch). "The first time he tries that fancy Dan stuff in this league," wrote one pro scout, "they'll cram the ball down his throat."[29]

One of those with doubts was Red Auerbach, who had recently replaced Julian as coach of the Boston Celtics. For Boston's first-round selection in the 1950 college draft, Auerbach chose Louisville center Chuck Share rather than the popular Cousy. When a reporter later questioned the move, the Boston coach explained his decision in no uncertain terms: "The only thing that counts with me is ability, and Cousy still hasn't proven to me that he's got that ability. I'm not interested in drafting someone just because he happens to be a local yokel."[30]

Cousy was eventually selected by the Tri-Cities Blackhawks with the ninth pick of the draft. Soon afterward he was traded to the Chicago Stags for forward Gene Vance. The financially troubled Chicago franchise soon folded, however. When a special dispersal draft was held, Cousy was awarded to the Celtics. He found himself with his third NBA team before having played a single game in the league.

Instant Stardom

Despite Auerbach's doubts about his ability, Cousy took the league by storm. As a rookie he finished ninth in scoring in the eleven-team circuit (second among the Celtics to Ed Macauley) and fourth in assists. He ran the team's fast-break offense like a veteran and helped the club to the first winning record in

Cousy dribbles past a St. Louis Hawks guard. As a rookie, Cousy ranked second among his teammates in scoring and fourth in assists.

franchise history (39-30). On March 2, 1951, Cousy was a member of the East squad that defeated the West, 111-94, in the first NBA All-Star Game. Playing before the hometown fans in Boston, he scored eight points, with nine rebounds and eight assists. It was the first of thirteen All-Star appearances for Cousy, one for each of his NBA seasons.

The Celtics added Bill Sharman in Cousy's second year in the league. Together, the two formed the league's foremost guard combination. Cousy raised his scoring average to a career-high 21.7 points per game while his assists increased to 6.7 per contest. The marks were third and second best in the league, respectively. Although the Celtics finished the year in second place, just one game behind Syracuse, the team was upset by the New York Knickerbockers in the first round of the playoffs for the second year in a row.

An Incredible Performance

By the time the 1952–53 season came to an end, Cousy had established himself as one of the game's greatest stars. He led the league in assists for the first of eight consecutive seasons while again finishing third in scoring. Boston finished with a 46-25 record and faced the Syracuse Nationals in the first round of the playoffs.

The Celtics won the first game in Syracuse 87-81. The two teams moved back to Boston for Game 2 where they battled evenly for forty-eight minutes. With two seconds left in regulation time, Cousy sank a free throw for his twenty-fifth point to tie the score and send the game into overtime.

The first extra period ended in the same manner, with Cousy again knotting the score on a free throw. Syracuse led by two with time running out in the second overtime, but Cousy's running hook shot tied the score once again, forcing a third extra period. This time, the Nationals led by five points with just thirteen seconds remaining. Cousy would not be denied, however. He was fouled while scoring on a drive and sank the free throw to complete a three-point play. A Syracuse turnover gave the Celtics one final chance and Cousy came through yet again. His wild shot from near midcourt found the mark to send the game into an unbelievable fourth overtime.

Cousy drives toward the basket in the 1953 playoffs against the Syracuse Nationals, scoring an astonishing fifty points in the second game of the series.

Cousy poured in nine more points in the fourth overtime to help Boston come from five points back. The Celtics won by a score of 111-105 to give them the first playoff series win in team history. Cousy had scored an incredible fifty points in the game—including twenty-five in the four extra periods—to set a new playoff record. His thirty free throws is a record that has stood for nearly half a century. Many observers considered his performance to be the greatest ever seen in a professional basketball game. It cemented his status as the greatest guard to play the sport.

The First Championship

The Celtics failed to get past the Eastern Division Finals in both 1953 and 1954. Cousy, however, was a model of consistency. He paced the Boston attack in scoring while amazing fans around the league with his ballhandling and passing. The potent Celtics offense consistently ranked at or near the top of the NBA. The problem was a weak defense.

All that changed in 1956 when the Celtics obtained center Bill Russell in the college draft. Russell's talents blended perfectly with Cousy's. A fierce rebounder, Russell quickly got the ball to Cousy, whose sharp passes to teammates cutting toward the hoop resulted in countless easy baskets. As teammate Tom Heinsohn recalls, "Cooz was the absolute offensive master. . . . Once that ball reached his hands, the rest of us just took off, never bothering to look back. We didn't have to. He'd find us. When you got into a position to score, the ball would be there."[31]

By All-Star time, the Celtics had established themselves as the dominant team in the league. Cousy scored 10 points and had five rebounds and seven assists in the midseason event to win the game's Most Valuable Player award for the second time. For the 1956–57 season, he averaged 20.6 points a game (eighth in the league) and led the NBA in assists for the fifth consecutive year. The Celtics compiled a 44-28 record for the best mark in the league. For his role in his team's success, Cousy was named the league's Most Valuable Player.

Boston proceeded to march through the playoffs. The Celtics defeated the St. Louis Hawks in an exciting finals series to win their first NBA championship. It would not be their last.

A Devastating Offense

Boston surrendered its crown to St. Louis the following season, but it would be Cousy's last year without a ring. The Celtics won the league championship in each of his last five seasons while establishing themselves as the greatest dynasty in the history of the sport.

Over this period Cousy was the ultimate point guard, directing the league's most potent attack. Some people, however, faulted him for his flashy ballhandling and passing, but Cousy defended his style: "I think I'm criticized unfairly. My trick plays serve two purposes . . . color helps build up a following . . . all my moves that look like showboating are made to keep the defense guessing and off-balance."[32]

The Celtics had no such complaints. They were in the top three in the league in scoring in every one of his thirteen NBA seasons except for his rookie year. On February 27, 1959, Boston set a record (since broken) by scoring 173 points in a game against the Minneapolis Lakers. Cousy's twenty-eight assists that night were also a new record, one which stood for nineteen years. His nineteen assists in one half is still a league mark. Later that year Cousy set a Boston playoff record by getting nineteen assists in Game 4 of the NBA Finals against Minneapolis. The Celtics won that game to give them a four-game sweep of the Lakers, the first such sweep in league finals history.

Coach Auerbach hugs Cousy at the end of the final game of the guard's very successful thirteen-year career.

The following season Cousy guided Boston to a 151-118 trouncing of the Cincinnati Royals on November 11. The Celtics set a team record that day by scoring ninety-one points in a single half. The Boston juggernaut raced through the league, compiling a record-tying seventeen-game winning streak before being stopped on New Year's Day 1960.

Cousy's burning desire to succeed helped make him one of the most popular Celtics in team history. When he announced in October 1962 that he would retire at the end of that season, plans were immediately made to honor New England's favorite son. Bob Cousy Day was celebrated on St. Patrick's Day, March 17, 1963, the date of the Celtics' final regular-season game. During an emotional ceremony, a tearful Cousy gave a heartfelt farewell speech. At the end, a voice from the Boston Gardens stands cried out, "We love ya, Cooz,"[33] bringing tears to the eyes of many spectators. (The game is still known as "the Boston Tear Party.")

Cousy's scoring average in his last season was a career-low 13.2 points per game. He still managed to lead the club to one final championship, however, as Boston defeated the Royals and Lakers in the playoffs to win their fifth consecutive title. In the last game of the finals series Cousy ended his career by dribbling out the last few seconds of the game. When the final buzzer sounded he tossed the ball toward the rafters in exultation.

After the Celtics

In the fall of 1963, at age thirty-five, Cousy embarked on a new career. Always a student of the game, he landed the head coaching job at Boston College. He guided the school to a 10-11 record in his first season in charge. Over the next five years the Eagles won an average of more than twenty-one games per season. As a result, the team made the postseason National Invitational Tournament (NIT) three times and the NCAA tournament twice. Cousy's cumulative record for six seasons at the helm was 117-38 for an excellent winning percentage of .755.

In 1969 Cousy left Boston College to return to the NBA, this time as coach of the Cincinnati Royals. "I did it for the money," he admitted. "I was made the offer I couldn't refuse."[34] Saddled with a slumping team, he even returned as a player for seven games in 1969–70 in an effort to spark the club. Unfortunately, he could not work his magic. He stepped down as coach in 1974 having compiled a 141-209 record in four and a half seasons.

Cousy ventured forth on yet another career that fall. He used his extensive knowledge of the game to become a successful analyst on Celtics television broadcasts. It was for his years as a player, however, that he was elected to the Basketball Hall of Fame in 1971. In addition to having scored nearly seventeen thousand points in his career, he had almost seven thousand assists. He was named to the All-NBA First Team for ten consecutive years and was selected for the twenty-fifth, thirty-fifth, and fiftieth NBA Anniversary All-Time Teams. His influence on the game was perhaps best put into words by Celtics owner

Cousy on the sidelines as head basketball coach of Boston College where he compiled an impressive record over six seasons.

Walter Brown at the time of Cousy's retirement. "The Celtics wouldn't be here without him. He made basketball in this town. I don't know but what he made basketball period. If he had played in New York he would have been the biggest thing since Babe Ruth."[35]

CHAPTER 4

Bill Russell

The word most often associated with Bill Russell is winner. He revolutionized the game of basketball by showing how defense could control the tempo of a game. Whether it was in college, the Olympics, or the pros, Russell was usually the dominant figure on the court, controlling play through his shot-blocking and rebounding.

A Difficult Childhood

William Felton Russell was born in Monroe, Louisiana, on February 12, 1934. His father, Charles, worked in a paper-bag factory. His mother, Katie, stayed home and took care of Bill, who was a sickly child, and his older brother, Charlie.

As a black youngster growing up in the Deep South, Bill was forced to face the reality of racial discrimination at an early age. One time, his father was threatened by a white man with a shotgun. Another time, his mother was threatened with jail because of the way she dressed. These events and others naturally made a deep impression on the child, but so, too, did his mother's advice. "William," she said, "you are going to meet people who just don't like you. On sight. And there's

48

nothing you can do about it, so don't worry. Just be yourself. You're no better than anyone else, but no one's better than you."[36]

When Bill was five years old Charles was denied a raise at the mill where he worked because of his color. He decided to move his family to Oakland, California, where he got a job in a war plant. For a while the Russells lived in a house Bill remembered as a "filthy hole."[37] Later they moved into an apartment in the city's projects. His parents eventually separated, and his mother died when he was twelve years old. Charles took the two boys back in with him, and Bill and his brother grew closer.

Bill started playing basketball at age nine. As a tall, skinny youngster at Oakland's Hoover Junior High School, he tried out for the basketball team but did not make it. Later, as a six-foot, two-inch, 128-pound sophomore at McClymonds High, Bill was the last player selected for the junior varsity squad. By the time he graduated in 1952, however, he had grown several inches, put on weight, and improved his skills to the point of being a valuable member of the team. He had intended to work in the local shipyards to save up enough money to go to college part time, but his plans changed when he was offered a scholarship to the University of San Francisco (USF).

Russell began his freshman year at USF in the fall of 1952. While there, he teamed with guard K.C. Jones under coach Phil Woolpert to help the Dons become a powerhouse. The small Jesuit school attracted national attention with a winning streak that eventually reached fifty-five games. In Russell's final two years (1954–55 and 1955–56), San Francisco was the nation's number one team. In both seasons the Dons won the postseason NCAA tournament. In 1955 Russell was named Most Outstanding Player of the Final Four when he pulled down twenty-five rebounds in the championship game against LaSalle. The next year, he scored twenty-six points and grabbed twenty-seven rebounds in a victory over Iowa that gave the Dons their second NCAA title. Russell won All-American recognition both years and left San Francisco as one of just five players to average twenty points and twenty rebounds per game in his collegiate career.

Bill Russell in midair after dunking the ball during an NCAA tournament semifinal game.

The Missing Piece

Following his graduation in 1956 Russell was drafted by the St. Louis Hawks of the NBA. Celtics coach Red Auerbach desperately wanted Russell, who he thought could be the player to turn Boston into a contending team. Other observers, however, questioned his ability to play in the pros. "Russell wasn't a scorer in college," said Philadelphia Warriors owner Eddie Gottlieb. "People say he can't shoot and can't score. What good is he?"[38]

To obtain the rights to the six-foot, nine-and-a-half-inch center, Auerbach traded high-scoring center Ed Macauley and rookie prospect Cliff Hagan to the Hawks. Before signing a contract, however, Russell earned a spot on the U.S. Olympic basketball team that competed in the 1956 Summer Games in Melbourne, Australia. Russell contributed to the team's 8-0 record and returned home with a gold medal. Ready to test himself in the NBA, he signed a contract with the Celtics for $19,500 and joined the team a third of the way through the season. He played his first game in a Boston uniform on December 26, 1956, in a nationally televised game against the St. Louis Hawks.

In previous years the Celtics had been a high-scoring team, but one that could not prevent the other team from putting points on the board. Russell's impact was immediate. No longer could opposing clubs drive down the middle for easy layups. Russell was an intimidating player whose jumping ability and quick reactions enabled him to block shot after shot. His rebounding and swift outlet passes triggered the vaunted Celtics fast break, which led to many easy baskets.

Russell played in only forty-eight games his rookie year, pulling down a league high of 19.6 rebounds per contest while scoring 14.7 points per game. The Celtics finished the regular season with the best record in the league and then defeated Syracuse and St. Louis in the playoffs to win their first NBA title. In the finals series against the Hawks, he set a rookie finals record by notching 22.9 rebounds per game. Although teammate Tom Heinsohn won Rookie of the Year honors, Russell's presence was of paramount importance to the team's success. He showed one and all that it was possible to be a pivotal player even without scoring a single point.

The next year the Celtics won their first fourteen games and never let up. Russell was a rebounding machine, leading the league with an average of 22.7 boards per contest. On November 16 he set an NBA record by getting thirty-two rebounds in the first half of a game against the Philadelphia Warriors. (To put that in perspective, no player reached thirty rebounds for an entire game in the 2000–01 season.) His importance to the team was recognized when he was named the league's Most Valuable Player for the first of five times.

The Celtics appeared on their way to a second consecutive championship after defeating the Warriors in the 1958 Eastern Division Finals. In Boston's Game 3 victory, Russell hauled down forty rebounds for a postseason club record. The team advanced to the finals series, where they met the Hawks in a replay of their matchup of the previous season.

With the series tied at one game apiece, Russell suffered a knee injury in Game 3. The Celtics lost the contest, then split the next two games without their star center. Russell returned to action in Game 5, but it was obvious he was not at full strength. Led by forward Bob Pettit's fifty

Russell (left) takes an elbow in the face from Wilt Chamberlain as he leaps to block a jump shot.

points, the Hawks held on to defeat the Celtics by one point to take the title.

The Rivalry

The Celtics were determined to regain the championship in 1958–59. They dominated the Eastern Division, finishing twelve games ahead of the runner-up New York Knicks. Russell raised his scoring and rebounding averages to 16.7 and 23.0, respectively. In the playoffs, Boston squeaked past Syracuse in seven games to move into the NBA Finals against the Lakers. There, Russell was unstoppable. He set an NBA Finals record for highest rebounds-per-game average with an amazing 29.5. The Celtics breezed past the Lakers in four straight games, giving them the first such sweep in NBA Finals history.

The Celtics were clearly the best team in professional basketball. In 1959, however, a new face emerged to challenge Russell as the league's dominant center. Seven-foot, one-inch rookie Wilt Chamberlain joined the Philadelphia Warriors and had an immediate effect on the league. In the first regular season meeting between the two players, Chamberlain outscored Russell 30-22, but Russell won the rebound battle 35-28. The Celtics emerged victorious by a score of 115-106.

The game established a pattern that would continue through the decade. Chamberlain often outscored and outrebounded his counterpart, but the Celtics won the majority of the games. In the ten seasons the pair faced each other, the Celtics compiled an 84-57 record against Chamberlain's teams. Russell won nine NBA championships over that period to one for Chamberlain. (Ironically, that one championship was in 1966–67, the first year that Wilt did not lead the league in scoring.)

In 1959–60 Boston finished ten games ahead of Philadelphia in the regular season. On February 5, 1960, Russell set an NBA record by grabbing fifty-one rebounds in a game against the Syracuse Nationals. (Chamberlain would break the mark the next season with fifty-five rebounds against the Celtics.) In the postseason Russell again was magnificent. In the deciding seventh game of the NBA Finals against the Hawks, he scored twenty-two points and collected thirty-five rebounds as Boston clinched its second title in a row with a 122-103 victory.

Aggressive moves, like this attempt to steal a rebound from Wilt Chamberlain, earned Russell (left) four NBA MVP awards.

A Decade of Dominance

With Russell anchoring the defense, the Celtics won the NBA title in each of the next six seasons. His value to the team is illustrated by the four Most Valuable Player awards he won in that span (1961, 1962, 1963, and 1965). When guards Bob Cousy and Bill Sharman retired, Sam Jones and John Havlicek took over the scoring burden on the team. The one constant was Russell in the middle. The guards were able to take chances on defense knowing that Russell was always there to cover their mistakes. Even if he did nothing, opposing players were always aware of him. As Ed Macauley explains, "I'm a shooter. . . . To be a great shooter you must be able to concentrate. There can be only one thing on your mind when you go up for a shot: the hoop. And this is where Russell changed things. Now you had two things to concentrate on: the hoop, and 'Where is he?'"[39]

In 1961–62 Chamberlain had the greatest offensive season of any player in history, winning the scoring title by averaging a mind-boggling 50.4 points per game. Cincinnati's Oscar Robertson achieved his remarkable triple-double that same season. When all was said and done, however, Russell was named the league's Most Valuable Player. He averaged a career-high 18.9 points per game while pulling down 23.6 rebounds per contest to help the Celtics to their fourth title in a row.

The following years saw Russell and the Celtics continue their domination of the league. Russell won his third consecutive Most Valuable Player trophy in 1962–63. The next year, he led the league in rebounds with a career high of 24.7 per game and anchored what he considered the best Boston team of his time. The Celtics crushed the Royals and Warriors in the playoffs, winning each best-of-seven series in just five games.

In 1964–65 Russell again won the rebounding crown. He averaged 24.1 per contest for the year and had a single-game high of 49 against the Pistons on March 11. His scoring average fell to 14.1 points per game, but he ranked fifth in the league in assists. No other center finished in the top ten.

In August 1965 Russell signed a new 1965–66 contract for $100,001. The extra dollar was added to make him the league's highest-paid player, ahead of Wilt Chamberlain, who had signed with Philadelphia for $100,000. The season was Red Auerbach's last as the team's coach, and Russell helped him go out a winner. He averaged 22.8 rebounds, 12.9 points, and 4.8 assists per game to help the Celtics reach the playoffs. Once there, he raised his game to another level. In leading Boston to wins over Cincinnati, Philadelphia, and Los Angeles, Russell increased his numbers to 25.2 rebounds, 19.1 points, and 5.0 assists a game. In the seventh and final game of the NBA Finals, he scored 25 points and grabbed 32 rebounds against the Lakers to help Boston to a 95-93 victory and an unprecedented eighth consecutive championship.

A First for Professional Sports

Following the Lakers' victory in Game 1 of the 1966 finals, Auerbach announced his successor as head coach of the Celtics. His choice was none other than Russell, who as player/coach thus

Russell launches a hook shot as Wilt Chamberlain goes up for the block.

became the first black coach of a major professional sports team. Russell's Boston teammates were pleased with his selection. "Russell is the team leader," said Frank Ramsey, "and has been all his time here. So it is only natural he becomes the coach."[40]

Not everyone, however, thought Russell had made the right decision in accepting the job. In January 1967, Wilt Chamberlain said of his longtime nemesis, "The stupidest thing he ever did was to coach. He ought to quit and go back to playing only."[41]

Nonetheless, Russell's Celtics improved their record by six games in his first season in charge. Unfortunately, Chamberlain's Philadelphia 76ers emerged as a new league powerhouse, winning a record sixty-eight games in the regular season against only thirteen defeats. When the two teams met in the Eastern Division Finals, the Celtics were no match for Philadelphia. The 76ers won the series, four games to one, to advance to the NBA Finals, where they defeated the San Francisco Warriors to take the NBA title.

The Celtics of 1967–68 were an aging crew with several key players closing in on retirement. The club won fifty-four games in the regular season, six fewer than the previous year. After beating the New York Knicks in the opening round of the playoffs, they faced the heavily favored 76ers in the Eastern Division Finals. After losing the opener, Philadelphia bounced back to take the next three games and a commanding lead. The Celtics, however, refused to lie down. They won the next two games to even the series and force a seventh game. In the deciding contest the Celtics led by two points with less than a minute left in the game. At that point Russell again raised his game a notch. He sank a free throw, blocked a shot, pulled down a rebound, and assisted on the final basket to help the Celtics score a 100-96 victory and take the series. With that win they became the first NBA team to come back from a deficit of three games to one in a postseason series.

In their return to the championship round, Boston eliminated the Lakers in six games to bring the title back to Boston and give Russell his first ring as coach. At the age of thirty-four he averaged 22.8 rebounds, 14.4 points, and 5.2 assists per game in nineteen playoff contests to spark Boston to the NBA crown.

At age thirty-five Russell finished third in the league in rebounding in 1968–69, averaging better than nineteen per game. His scoring, however, fell to a career-low 9.9 points per contest. Boston finished the year in fourth place in the Eastern Division and seemed headed for an early exit in the playoffs.

Russell, however, had one final bit of magic left. He led the Celtics to upset victories over the 76ers and Knicks to put Boston in the NBA Finals one more time. There, they met the Los Angeles Lakers, who had acquired Chamberlain from the 76ers the previous year. In their final encounter, Russell again came out on top. He led the Celtics to a hard-fought win in the seven-game series for his eleventh championship in thirteen NBA seasons. It was a fitting ending to the most successful career in pro basketball history.

A Complex Human Being

A well-read and outspoken individual, Russell never hesitated to speak his mind, which occasionally hurt his popularity. He was critical of fans who worshiped ballplayers and refused to give autographs, even to teammates. Acutely aware of racial injustice, Russell was never as popular as some of his white teammates in Boston, a city he referred to in his book *Second Wind* as "a flea market of racism. It had all varieties, old and new, and in their most virulent form."[42]

Russell's candor helped win him favorable reviews in his next job as a color analyst on ABC's weekly pro basketball telecasts. As one writer related in a 1972 review in *Life*, "Russell's commentary on the last six NBA games has been as loose, confident, skillful, and precise as his play at center for the Celtics. You know exactly when he's disgusted, exactly when he's bemused, exactly when he's bored."[43]

The following summer Russell accepted the job of head coach and general manager of the struggling Seattle SuperSonics. In his second year in charge, the team made the playoffs for the first time in its eight-year existence. He left Seattle after four seasons, then returned to the NBA eleven years later for a brief, unsuccessful stint as head coach of the Sacramento Kings.

Numerous honors have come Russell's way since he retired as a player. In 1974 he was elected to the Naismith Memorial

Coach Auerbach congratulates Bill Russell for his central role in the Celtics championship team. Russell has been voted the Greatest Player in the History of the NBA.

Basketball Hall of Fame. Six years later he was voted the Greatest Player in the History of the NBA by the Professional Basketball Writers Association of America. Although some may argue that Michael Jordan, Oscar Robertson, or Wilt Chamberlain has equaled him on the court, none can argue with another designation often attached to his name. His place as basketball's ultimate winner is unassailable. "I played because I enjoyed it," he explains, "but there's more to it than that. I played because I was dedicated to being the best. I was part of a team, and I dedicated myself to making that team the best."[44]

CHAPTER 5

John Havlicek

Perhaps the most famous basketball call of all time was made by Boston Celtics announcer Johnny Most at the end of the seventh game of the 1965 Eastern Division Finals between Boston and the Philadelphia 76ers. With the Celtics ahead by one point and just five seconds left to play, Boston's John Havlicek deflected Philadelphia's inbounds pass to save the victory. The move prompted Most's legendary, "Havlicek stole the ball! . . . Havlicek stole the ball!"[45] The play was a perfect example of how Havlicek always seemed to come through when the game was on the line. He was one of the greatest clutch performers in the history of the NBA and arguably the greatest hustler the game has ever seen.

Life in the Valley

John J. Havlicek was born in Lansing, Ohio, on April 8, 1940. He was the third of Frank and Mandy Havlicek's four children. John has an older brother and sister, and a younger sister who died when she was five years old. His father came to America from Czechoslovakia when he was twelve years old. His mother, of Croatian descent, was born in the United States. The couple owned a grocery store in Lansing, so although they struggled to support their children, there was always food on the table.

As a youngster John had to make do without many of the extras enjoyed by other kids in his neighborhood in the Upper Ohio Valley. While most of his friends had bicycles, he was forced to run after them when they went out riding. John credited this for helping him develop the stamina that was a major asset to him as a player.

Sports were an important recreation in the valley. Several professional athletes came from the region, including football notables Clarke Hinkle, Lou Groza, and Chuck Howley; basketball star Alex Groza; and baseball major leaguers Bill Mazeroski and Joe and Phil Niekro, who lived across the street from the Havliceks. (John and Phil were "as close as two kids growing up together can be," says Phil. "We did everything as a pair."[46]) Like most boys in the valley, John was active in sports year-round.

At Bridgeport High School, John was involved in all sports. "He was just an outstanding all-around high school athlete,"[47] says Phil Niekro. John played all four infield positions and batted cleanup on the baseball team. He hit well over .400 in both his junior and senior seasons and attracted attention from scouts for the Baltimore Orioles, Cincinnati Reds, Cleveland Indians, Pittsburgh Pirates, and New York Yankees. He also starred in football as a strong-armed quarterback and received scholarship offers from numerous colleges.

Basketball, however, was his favorite sport. The fast-break offense of coach Bobby Carroll was perfectly suited to John. He averaged nearly thirty-three points per game as a six-foot one-inch junior. The next year, after growing two inches, he averaged thirty points and twenty rebounds per contest.

As a senior he became the first youngster from the region to be named All-State in all three sports. Although many observers thought he was making a mistake, John decided to accept a basketball scholarship to Ohio State. As one local writer said, "Taking nothing away from John's basketball ability, we still think he's a better football player. Passers like Havlicek come along once in a blue moon."[48]

Legendary Ohio State football coach Woody Hayes tried to get John to go out for the football team, but without success.

Ohio State football coach Woody Hayes (pictured) tried unsuccessfully to persuade John Havlicek to play football instead of basketball.

Referring to Havlicek, he was often heard to say, "The best quarterback in the Big Ten isn't playing football."[49]

Although John never played football for the Buckeyes, pro scouts did not forget him. He would be selected by the Cleveland Browns in the 1962 college draft and sign a contract with them for $15,000. Because of his speed and sure hands, they switched him to end. John appeared in one exhibition game and was the team's last cut prior to the beginning of the regular season. He had fine skills, and he was very competitive, recalls Browns star Lou Groza, "but he hadn't played in so long that the things we did naturally, he had to think about."[50]

National Champions

At Ohio State, Havlicek's freshman basketball team included future NBA players Jerry Lucas and Mel Nowell and future Indiana University head coach Bobby Knight. As sophomores they moved up to the varsity (freshmen could not play varsity ball at the time), where they joined junior Larry Siegfried and senior Joe Roberts, two others who would one day play in the NBA. Fred Taylor was the team's head coach.

Havlicek became a starter in the second game of his sophomore season. In a contest against the University of Michigan he hit all nine of his shots, setting a school single-game record for shooting that still stands. The Buckeyes lost only two games that year and made it to the postseason NCAA tournament. There they defeated Western Kentucky, Georgia Tech, and New York University (whose star was Havlicek's future Celtics teammate Tom Sanders) to advance to the championship game against the University of California. There the sophomore-dominated squad completed their run to the top, defeating California by a score of 75-55. The twenty-point margin of victory was, at the time, the largest in an NCAA championship contest.

The next year Ohio State breezed through the regular season without a loss. In the NCAA tournament the Buckeyes again made it to the final game. This time, however, they were defeated in overtime by a powerful University of Cincinnati squad for their only loss of the year. The two teams met in a rematch of the final game in 1962. Cincinnati again emerged victorious, giving Ohio State its second loss of the year against twenty-six wins.

Ohio State's record in Havlicek's three seasons was an outstanding 78-6. He averaged 14.6 points and 8.6 rebounds a game for his college career, played outstanding defense, and earned All-American honors as a senior. It was during this period that he acquired the nickname of Hondo, given to him by Mel Nowell, who had trouble pronouncing Havlicek. One day, Nowell decided Havlicek looked like rugged actor John Wayne and gave him the nickname in honor of a Wayne movie in theaters at the time.

A Key Reserve

Following his graduation in 1962, Havlicek was selected by the Celtics in the first round of the NBA draft. He was also picked by the Cleveland Pipers of the short-lived American Basketball League (ABL). After his tryout with the football Browns, he signed with the Celtics for $15,000. Boston had won the last four NBA titles and was set at all five starting positions. Coach Red Auerbach hoped Havlicek could develop into a solid reserve who might eventually replace Frank Ramsey in the sixth-man role on the team.

Havlicek began the year on the bench but saw more and more playing time as the season wore on. With his unselfish attitude, he was a perfect fit for the team-oriented Celtics, and his enthusiasm and intensity gave the veteran club a boost. Havlicek finished the year averaging 14.3 points and 6.7 rebounds per game. He earned a championship ring as a rookie as the Celtics won their fifth title in a row.

Havlicek releases a jump shot against the Los Angeles Lakers. Havlicek was a first-round pick for the Celtics in the 1962 draft.

Havlicek earned NBA All-Rookie Team honors for 1962–63, but there were still those who questioned his chances for a long career in the league. According to an article in *Sports Illustrated*, guard Bob Cousy thought he might just be a "non-shooter who would probably burn himself out."[51] Havlicek would soon prove him wrong.

When Cousy retired following the 1962–63 season, Havlicek took on a more important role in Boston's offense. He performed a rare feat the next year by leading the team in scoring as a reserve. He finished tenth in the league in scoring (19.9 points per game) and made the All-NBA Second Team. The Celtics repeated as champions and Havlicek solidified his reputation as the best nonstarter in basketball.

"Havlicek stole the ball!"

When the Celtics began the 1964–65 season by winning their first eleven games, it appeared no one would stand in the way of a seventh straight championship. They finished the year with the league's best record, fourteen games ahead of the second-place Cincinnati Royals in the Eastern Division.

Havlicek steals the ball from Philadelphia in the 1965 NBA division finals.

In the division finals, however, they found themselves locked in a struggle with the Philadelphia 76ers. The two teams took turns winning the first six games of the series, setting up a seventh and deciding meeting. With five seconds remaining in the contest, Boston led by a single point, 110-109. The Celtics had control of the ball, but Bill Russell's inbounds pass hit one of the wires that supported the basket, giving the ball back to Philadelphia. The 76ers had one last chance for a game-winning basket to end the Celtics streak and put Philadelphia into the NBA Finals.

Philadelphia guard Hal Greer prepared to put the ball into play from underneath his own basket. The logical move was to get the ball to high-scoring center Wilt Chamberlain for the last shot, but Chamberlain was well covered by Russell. Greer saw forward Chet Walker free out past the key (the top of the free throw circle). He threw a pass in that direction, but Havlicek anticipated the play. Boston broadcaster Johnny Most described the action to his radio audience: "Greer is putting the ball into play. He gets it out deep." Suddenly his voice rose in excitement. "Havlicek steals it. Over to Sam Jones. Havlicek stole the ball! It's all over! Johnny Havlicek stole the ball!"[52] His description of the play has become the most famous radio call in basketball history.

The Sixth Man

Over the next two seasons Havlicek cemented his reputation as a supersub, the best sixth man in the history of the NBA. He accepted the role without complaint. "It never bothered me," he once explained, "because I think that role is very important to a club. One thing I learned from Red Auerbach was that it's not who starts the game, but who finishes it, and I generally was around at the finish."[53]

Havlicek blossomed into an excellent shooter who could be counted on for twenty-plus points per night. He was hard for opposing players to defend against because at six feet, five inches and 205 pounds, he was bigger than most guards and quicker than most forwards. His constant movement enabled him to wear down opposing players. (It was once estimated that he ran between three and five miles during the course of a single game.)

Havlicek's rebounding and passing also improved. His rebound totals increased each year from 1965 to 1971, while his assists went up every year from 1965 to 1972. Boston was still winning (having taken the NBA championship in 1966 and 1968), but the team was showing signs of aging. The Celtics finished in fourth place in 1968–69, but surprised everyone in the playoffs by winning their tenth title in eleven seasons. Bill Russell's retirement following the end of the season marked the end of an era.

That summer Havlicek received an offer from the Carolina Cougars of the new American Basketball Association (ABA). Although Carolina offered him more money, he re-signed with the Celtics rather than uproot his family and start over in a new

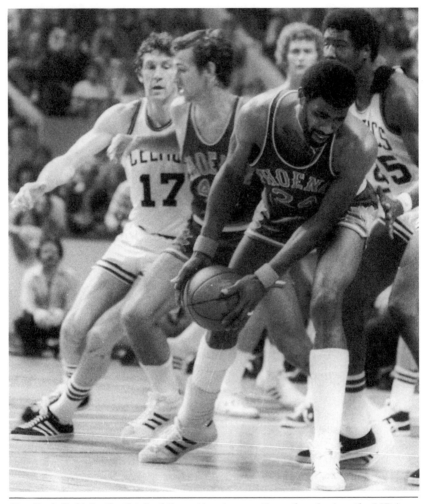

Havlicek (left) in the thick of the action in overtime play during the NBA playoffs.

city. With a three-year, $400,000 contract in his pocket, Havlicek responded with the three best years—statistically—of his career. He recorded his top three totals in points, rebounds, and assists over that span. Unfortunately, with Russell out of the picture, the Celtics struggled. They finished out of the playoffs in both 1969–70 and 1970–71 before bouncing back to win the Eastern Division in 1971–72.

Back to the Top

Despite having turned thirty years old during the 1969–70 season, Havlicek showed no sign of slowing down. As the recognized leader of the team, he was named captain, a title he would retain for the remainder of his career. Havlicek led the league in minutes played each of the next two years. In 1970–71 he finished second in the league in scoring and fourth in assists. The following year he finished third in scoring and fifth in assists.

By that time, center Dave Cowens and guard Jo Jo White had established themselves as productive NBA players. The Celtics finished first in the Eastern Division in 1972–73 with a franchise-best record of 68-14. In the Eastern Division Finals, they faced the New York Knicks, who had eliminated them in the same round of the playoffs the previous year.

The two clubs split the first two games, but Havlicek suffered a severe shoulder separation and tearing of the joint capsule in Game 3. He returned to action in Game 5 with the Celtics down three games to one. Shooting mostly left-handed because of his injury, Havlicek scored eighteen points and led Boston to a one-point victory. The Celtics managed to win Game 6 to tie the series, but with Havlicek still hurting, they lost the final game—and the series—to New York.

After their near miss in 1972–73, the Celtics made it all the way back to the top the next season. Havlicek led the team in scoring for a sixth straight year. On January 11, in a game against the Lakers, he scored the twenty thousandth point of his NBA career.

In the playoffs that spring Havlicek led Boston past the Buffalo Braves and New York Knicks to get to the NBA Finals. Playing Kareem Abdul-Jabbar and the Milwaukee Bucks, the Celtics took the series in seven exciting games to give them the championship. Havlicek was the club's dominant player. He averaged 27.1 points per game and was named NBA Finals Most Valuable Player. The victory was especially sweet since it was Boston's first without Bill Russell at the center position. In the locker room after the game, the usually unemotional Havlicek was ecstatic. "Thanks for doing this for me," he told his teammates. "This is the greatest one."[54]

The Greatest Game Ever?

Havlicek made it back to the NBA Finals one more time as an active player. In 1975–76 the Celtics defeated Buffalo and the Cleveland Cavaliers to advance to the championship series against the Phoenix Suns. Boston won in six games to give Havlicek his eighth—and final—ring. Game 5 of the 1976 NBA Finals is considered by many to be the greatest game ever played.

With the series tied at two games apiece, the teams returned to Boston on June 4. Regulation time ended with the score tied. Likewise, the first overtime period also ended with the two teams even. With just four seconds left in the second extra period, Havlicek drove the length of the floor and scored on an off-balance fifteen-foot shot to give Boston a 110-109 lead as time appeared to have run out. Fans poured out onto the floor, but the referees ruled that Phoenix's Paul Westphal (a former Celtic) had called time-out with two seconds remaining. The Suns, however, did not have any time-outs left. The shrewd move by Westphal resulted in a technical foul that the Celtics converted for a two-point lead. However, because of the technical, the Suns were given the ball at midcourt rather than under their own basket. Phoenix forward Garfield took the inbounds pass, turned, and threw up a desperation shot that miraculously went in to stun the Boston Garden crowd and send the game into a third overtime period. This time the Celtics took the lead and managed to hold on. They emerged with a 128-126 victory, then won two days later to take the title.

The Hall of Famer

Havlicek played his final NBA game on April 9, 1978. His uniform number 17 was retired the next October before a game with the Cavaliers. He left the game with a long list of accomplishments and honors. In addition to being a thirteen-time NBA All-Star, he was also a member of the All-NBA Defensive First Team five times. At the time of his retirement Havlicek ranked third in league history in field goals attempted, fourth in minutes played, sixth in games played, seventh in field goals made, and ninth in scoring. In addition, he topped the list of all-time Celtics in games played, minutes played, points, field

Havlicek proudly displays a ball indicating that he has surpassed the 25,000-career-point mark, only the fourth player in NBA history to do so.

goals attempted and made, and free throws attempted and made. He was also the first person in history to score one thousand points in sixteen consecutive seasons. Considering that he was not a starter for a good portion of his career, these achievements are all the more amazing.

In 1983 Havlicek was elected to the Naismith Memorial Basketball Hall of Fame. Thirteen years later he was named to the NBA 50th Anniversary All-Time Team. His eight championship rings have been matched by only Bill Russell (thirteen), Sam Jones (ten), Tom Sanders (eight), and K.C. Jones (eight). It is no wonder that Red Auerbach has often described him as "the measure of what it means to be a Celtic."[55]

CHAPTER 6

Dave Cowens

Dave Cowens earned a reputation as a blue-collar player, displaying traits rarely seen in a player his size. Standing six feet, nine inches tall, he dominated players several inches taller at the center position through sheer hustle and desire. A seven-time All-Star, Cowens was named one of the NBA's top fifty players of all time. "I never considered myself a superstar," he said after his selection to the Hall of Fame in 1990. "I feel I represent the working class of the NBA."[56]

An Intense Competitor

David William Cowens was born on October 25, 1948, in Newport, Kentucky, just across the Ohio River from the city of Cincinnati. His father was a barber who struggled to provide for his wife and six children.

Northern Kentucky is noted for tobacco, horse racing, and basketball. Dave was introduced to the sport at the age of eight. At St. Anthony's elementary school, he was smaller than some of the other boys but made up for his lack of size with his scrappiness. Said St. Anthony's coach Jim Callahan, "If Dave hadn't been so competitive, he might not have made the team."[57]

71

Dave enjoyed playing all sports and made the football, track, and swimming teams at Newport Catholic High School as a five-foot, eleven-inch freshman. When he shot up five inches by his sophomore year, he decided to try out for the basketball team. By his junior season Dave was starting at forward for the Thoroughbreds. He averaged 9.7 points per game that year, but rebounding was his specialty. His great leaping ability helped him finish second on the team in rebounds as Newport compiled a record of 21-8.

In Dave's senior year he scored 13.5 points per game while leading the team in rebounds. He set school records for a single season and a career in that important category. He received scholarship offers from several schools in the area, but he was not pursued by legendary coach Adolph Rupp of the University of Kentucky. Partly because of this snub Dave eventually decided to enroll at Florida State University (FSU). This was a bold move on his part for several reasons. First, FSU was better known as a football school and had not produced many NBA-level basketball players. Second, at the time, the school was on probation for recruiting violations and would not be eligible to play in any postseason tournaments in 1969 or 1970. Finally,

The entrance to Florida State University, where Dave Cowens had a successful college basketball career.

Dave's father, among others, had wanted him to attend a school closer to home in Kentucky.

One of the main reasons Dave chose FSU was the school's assistant coach, Hugh Durham. Durham vigorously pursued Cowens after finding out about him from Newport Catholic coach Jim Connor. Durham attended several of Dave's games and was bowled over by the youngster's talent. "The thing that impressed me most about Dave was his strength and quickness," said Durham. "Plus he played hard. And he played hard even though he didn't get the ball very much. You don't run across kids like that in high school very often."[58]

Durham stressed that FSU was looking for a strong rebounder. Although freshmen were not allowed to play on the varsity squad, Dave would likely be a starter as a sophomore. Cowens also liked the fact that the young, enthusiastic Durham was from Kentucky and had been a starting guard at FSU.

Cowens led FSU's freshman team to a 17-2 record in 1966–67. That same year Durham was named the school's head coach. When Cowens moved up to the varsity squad, he quickly became an important part of the team. He was an unselfish player who did whatever was necessary to help his club win. He improved his ballhandling and shooting skills and for the first time began to consider the possibility of playing professional ball after college. He began to work out with weights. By the time he was a senior, he was a muscular 227 pounds.

Cowens averaged eighteen points a game in his three years at Florida State, making 52 percent of his shots. He finished in the top ten nationally in rebounds each year, and was his team's Most Valuable Player three times. "There may be better shooters, better rebounders, better defensive players," said Durham, "but I doubt there is anyone who can do as many things as well as Dave."[59]

That opinion was shared by many of the pro scouts who followed him through his three years at FSU. For some the only question was what position he would play in the pros. At six feet, nine inches, he was short for a center. Some felt his outside shooting might not be good enough for a forward. The Celtics, however, thought he was too good to pass up.

Cowens stretches with a seemingly elastic reach to steal a rebound from a New Jersey Nets defender.

Filling Russell's Shoes

When Bill Russell retired from the Celtics following the 1968–69 championship season, he left a void that was not easily filled. Seven-footer Henry Finkel inherited his spot in the starting lineup but left much to be desired. He could not adequately compete with the league's top centers, Wilt Chamberlain, Bob Lanier, Nate Thurmond, Willis Reed, and Lew Alcindor (later Kareem Abdul-Jabbar). Boston finished in sixth place in the Eastern Division the next year with the franchise's first losing record—and first time finish out of the playoffs—in two decades.

It was obvious to head coach Tom Heinsohn what was missing. "We needed a big man," says Heinsohn. "We needed someone with speed, strength, and shooting ability to take our fast break and jam it down everyone's throat."[60]

Boston general manager Red Auerbach knew Cowens was the player he wanted. According to one story, when Auerbach first saw Cowens play, he stormed out of the gym, apparently annoyed by having wasted his time scouting the youngster but in reality, trying to trick other teams into thinking the Celtics were not interested. The Celtics eventually selected Cowens with the fourth overall pick in the 1970 NBA draft.

Auerbach loved Cowens's desire and work ethic, although he did not know whether Cowens was a center or a forward. As he explained at the time, "He's a very dedicated kid. A dedicated kid isn't unheard of, but there aren't as many around as we would like. But our problem with Cowens is telling him when to lay off. He does too much."[61]

Cowens was also drafted by the Miami team in the American Basketball Association. The new league could not entice him, however. He signed a contract with the Celtics for $300,000 over three years.

Cowens burst onto the NBA scene. In his first game he scored 16 points and grabbed 17 rebounds against the champion New York Knicks. He started the year playing more at forward and then gradually moved into the center position. He averaged 17.0 points and 15.4 rebounds a game in 1970–71 to share the league's Rookie of the Year honors with Geoff Petrie of the Portland Trail Blazers. His hustle and aggressiveness made

*Cowens grabs a rebound in midair against the Buffalo Braves. He averaged
13.6 rebounds a game for his career.*

him popular with Boston fans but occasionally got him into trouble: Cowens led the league with 350 personal fouls as a rookie. Although the Celtics showed a ten-game improvement in the regular season, they finished out of the playoffs for the second year in a row.

In just his first year in the league Cowens was already re-defining the center position. Most centers stationed themselves close to the basket and remained in the area to take advantage of their height, but Cowens was always moving around. With his outside shooting ability, he forced opposing centers to play farther from the basket in order to guard him. He ran the floor like a guard and chased after players much smaller than he was. Despite his success he knew he still had far to go.

A Perennial All-Star

Cowens spent the summer following his rookie year complet-ing the courses he needed to finish his degree in criminology from Florida State. He also worked at improving his game and the results were immediately evident. He played with a great deal more confidence and poise as he led the Celtics back to the top of the Atlantic Division. For his efforts he was named the starting center for the East in the midseason All-Star Game. Playing against Abdul-Jabbar and Chamberlain, Cowens scored fourteen points and pulled down twenty rebounds. He would be elected to six more All-Star games before retiring as an active player.

Cowens showed improvement in most statistical categories in 1971–72. His scoring average went up to 18.8 points per game, his field goal percentage rose to .484, and he finished fifth in the league in rebounds. Unfortunately, Boston was eliminated by New York in the second round of the playoffs.

The following season was statistically Cowens's best. He improved his outside shot even more and teamed with newly acquired forward Paul Silas to give Boston arguably the best rebounding duo in the league. Opposing players appreciated Cowens's distinctive style of play. "I can't recall anyone as active as Cowens," said New York Knicks forward Jerry Lucas. "He's perpetual motion. He runs on every play. He's all over the place. He switches out. He plays great defense. He's quick."[62]

The Celtics won their first ten games of the season. By the All-Star break they were in first place with a record of 39-7. During the midseason classic Cowens scored fifteen points and collected thirteen rebounds to lead his East squad to a 104-84 victory over the West. For his work, he was named the game's Most Valuable Player.

Boston went on to compile a dazzling 68-14 mark for the year. Averaging nearly forty-two minutes per game, Cowens recorded a career-high 20.5 points and 16.2 rebounds per contest. In a vote of the league players he joined Bob Cousy and Bill Russell in becoming the third Celtic to be named Most Valuable Player. "Being named MVP by my peers meant a lot to me," he later recalled. "I was always out to gain the respect of the players. They are the only ones who understand your work habits."[63]

Unfortunately for the Celtics, the team's performance in the playoffs was a repeat of the previous year. Boston again defeated the Atlanta Hawks in the conference semifinals and then lost to New York in the second round. Cowens took the loss hard. "No matter what we did this year," he said, "this means we didn't have a good season. When you go home a loser, you're left with a lousy feeling all the rest of the season. It's just sickening, that's what it is."[64]

A Thrilling Championship

After the disappointment of the previous season the Celtics were hungry for a championship in 1973–74. They began the year by winning twenty-nine of their first thirty-five games and went on to win the Atlantic Division by a seven-game margin. Cowens again dominated, averaging 19.0 points, 15.7 rebounds, and 4.4 assists per game.

In the playoffs the Celtics defeated the Braves in six games and the Knicks in five to advance to the NBA Finals, where they faced Kareem Abdul-Jabbar and the Milwaukee Bucks. The seven-foot, two-inch Abdul-Jabbar presented a problem for every opposing center. The Bucks plan was to get the ball to him as much as possible so he could shoot over the five-inch-shorter Cowens. The Celtics, for their part, wanted Cowens to draw Abdul-Jabbar away from the basket with his outside shooting while the rest of the team used a pressure defense to force the Bucks into mistakes.

Boston's strategy worked in the first game as the Celtics won 98-83. Cowens had difficulty hitting his outside shots in Game 2 and the Bucks evened the series. The two teams continued to alternate wins, and after five contests the Celtics were up three games to two.

In the dramatic sixth game the Bucks got Cowens into early foul trouble and built up a fourteen-point lead. The Celtics came back, however, and a Cowens jump shot with just over one minute remaining tied the score at eighty-six apiece. Regulation time ended with the score still tied and the game went into overtime. The first extra period ended at 90-90, forcing a second overtime. With just seven seconds left to play, Boston held a one-point lead. Milwaukee, however, managed to get the ball to Abdul-Jabbar. His last-second hook shot went in and gave the Bucks a 102-101 win to force a seventh game.

The two teams battled back and forth in the final contest with Cowens keeping Abdul-Jabbar in check. The Celtics eventually began to pull away, opening up a double-digit lead. With Cowens emerging as the game's leading scorer (twenty-eight points) and rebounder (fourteen boards), Boston won by a score of 102-87 to give them their first championship since Bill Russell's retirement.

The Quest for a Second Ring

The Celtics were favored to repeat as champs the next year, but before the regular season even began, misfortune struck. Cowens was injured during an exhibition game, fracturing a bone in his right foot. He missed the first seventeen games of the season as the team struggled to stay above .500.

When Cowens returned to action, he was unstoppable. He led the Celtics to fifty-one wins over their last sixty-five games to tie them with the Washington Bullets for the best record in the league. Cowens averaged 20.4 points and 14.7 rebounds per game and made the NBA All-Defensive Second Team. Thanks to his inspired play, Boston again finished in first place. Coach Tom Heinsohn recognized his contribution: "For three

Cowens takes a jump shot over the heads of three Philadelphia 76ers defenders.

months, Cowens played the best basketball any human has played in the NBA. He brought us to the top."[65] Cowens's all-out style of play, however, finally caught up with him. He appeared tired in the playoffs as the Celtics lost to the Bullets in the conference finals.

In an effort to take some of the offensive burden off Cowens, the Celtics traded for high-scoring Charlie Scott before the next season began. With Scott added to the cast, Boston raced to its fifth consecutive Atlantic Division crown. Cowens had one of his best all-around years, even though he was slowed by an assortment of nagging injuries. He rested most of the last two weeks of the season and came back to help Boston defeat Buffalo and Cleveland in the playoffs. The victories put the Celtics in the NBA Finals, where they faced Scott's former team, the Phoenix Suns. There Cowens paced the club to victory in an exciting six-game series. The Celtics had regained the title, the thirteenth in the franchise's history.

When One Door Closes . . .

Although Cowens played four more seasons with Boston, the team could not match its success of 1975–76. After his good friend Paul Silas was traded, Cowens seemed to lose some of his passion for the game. He announced his retirement at age twenty-eight and missed more than a third of the 1976–77 season before returning to action.

The Celtics were beginning a downward spiral that would see their win total drop from fifty-four in their championship season to forty-four to thirty-two. Although Cowens averaged more than sixteen points and eleven rebounds a game over that span, he never returned to top form.

When Boston got off to a 2-12 start in 1978–79, Cowens was hired as the team's player-coach (replacing Tom Sanders, who had taken over for Heinsohn the previous season). Cowens was in over his head, however. "I never had any coaching experience prior to that," he recalls. "It was too much for me."[66] He finished out the year before turning over control of the team to Bill Fitch. With the aid of rookie Larry Bird, Fitch helped bring the Celtics back to first place in 1979–80, Cowens's last season with the team.

. . . Another One Opens

After two seasons away from the NBA, Cowens returned as an active player briefly in 1982–83. Former teammate Don Nelson asked him to come out of retirement to play for Milwaukee, where Nelson was coaching at the time. The Bucks obtained him from Boston in exchange for guard Quinn Buckner in September. Cowens retired for the third and final time after the regular season.

Two years later Cowens got another taste of coaching, leading the Bay State club of the Continental Basketball Association (CBA). He made it back to the NBA in 1994 as an assistant coach under Bob Hill with the San Antonio Spurs. He left San Antonio after two seasons when he was offered the head coaching job with the Charlotte Hornets.

After retiring as a player, Cowens served two seasons as head coach of the Charlotte Hornets.

Cowens led the Hornets to back-to-back fifty-win seasons in his first two years at the helm. The team's 54-28 record in 1996-97 was the best mark in the franchise's history. For his efforts Cowens finished second in the voting for NBA Coach of the Year. Cowens stepped down after fifteen games in the lockout-delayed 1998–99 season but soon joined Garry St. Jean's staff with the Golden State Warriors. He was named head coach for the 2000–01 season. Unfortunately, the team was struck by a series of injuries and struggled all season. Cowens was fired in December 2001, leaving with a record of 25-80 over two seasons.

In eleven NBA seasons Cowens averaged 17.6 points and 13.6 rebounds a game. In eighty-nine playoff games, his averages increased to 18.9 and 14.4, respectively. Although his numbers are quite respectable, they do not adequately reflect his impact on professional basketball in the 1970s. The energy and enthusiasm he brought to the game have rarely been matched on the basketball court. He was named to the Basketball Hall of Fame in 1990 and to the NBA 50th Anniversary All-Time Team in 1996.

CHAPTER 7

Larry Bird

Larry Bird is arguably the greatest forward to play in the NBA. He excelled in all areas of play—scoring, rebounding, passing, and defending. He is also one of the greatest clutch players of all time, coming through in pressure situations time and time again. As Commissioner David Stern says, "Larry Bird has helped define the way a generation of basketball fans has come to view and appreciate the NBA."[67]

A Country Boy from Indiana

Larry Joe Bird, considered by some to be the most complete player of the modern era, was born in the small southern Indiana town of West Baden on December 7, 1956. The fourth of Joe and Georgia Bird's six children, Larry was a big baby, weighing eleven pounds, twelve ounces and measuring twenty-three inches at birth. Joe was a laborer, and his wife worked as a waitress in local restaurants to help make ends meet. Although born in West Baden, Larry grew up in nearby French Lick.

The Bird family was poor, and his parents struggled to put food on the table for their five sons and daughter. Larry was active in all sports, but basketball quickly became his favorite. Little did he know that his love for the game would someday bring him the riches he often dreamed of.

Larry played basketball whenever and wherever he could. As he later recalled, "I played when I was cold and my body was aching and I was so tired. . . . I didn't know why, I just kept playing and playing. . . . I guess I always wanted to make the most out of it. I just never knew it."[68] When he entered Spring Valley High School in French Lick as a six-foot, one-inch freshman in 1970, he made the baseball team as a pitcher. He decided to concentrate on basketball, however, and made the team as a guard in his sophomore year. When he broke his ankle two games into the season, he insisted on practicing his shooting and passing skills while recuperating. By Larry's senior year he had grown six inches and improved tremendously. As coach Gary Holland recalls, he was "definitely the best player [Holland] had ever coached."[69] Bird averaged 30.8 points and 20 rebounds a game that season and earned all-star recognition.

College coaches from around the country came calling on him, but the shy youngster wanted to remain close to home. He enrolled at the University of Indiana to play basketball under legendary coach Bobby Knight, but was quickly overwhelmed by the school's size. Coming from a town of just over two thousand, he felt lost among the thirty-three thousand students. He left school less than a month into the year and enrolled at Northwood Institute, a small junior college in West Baden. "People naturally think it was trouble between Knight and me," says Bird, "but it wasn't. The school was just too big. I was a homesick kid who was lost and broke."[70]

Bird did not last much longer at Northwood. He dropped out of school and took a job with the City Department in French Lick. His duties included maintaining area parks and roads and collecting garbage once a week. He enjoyed the work. "I loved that job," said Bird. "It was outdoors, you were around your friends. Picking up brush, cleaning up. I felt like I was really accomplishing something. . . . I had the chance to make my community look better."[71]

Sycamore All-American

The year 1975 was a particularly significant one in Bird's life. In early February tragedy touched the teenager. His father, who had divorced his mother two years earlier, had become despondent over financial problems. "I am not going to be around much longer," he told his kids. "No use me living this way. You kids would be better off if I was gone."[72] Sometime later, after telling his former wife of his plans on the phone, he picked up a shotgun and killed himself.

Larry Bird takes a jump shot as a star forward for Indiana State.

During this difficult period Bird was urged to go back to school by Bob King and Bill Hodges, the head coach and assistant coach at Indiana State University in Terre Haute. According to his mother, the school had been his first choice before he decided to attend Indiana. He eventually accepted a basketball scholarship and enrolled in 1975. NCAA transfer rules forced Bird to sit out a year before being allowed to play. (The year ended on a high note when he married Janet Condra, whom he had known since the first grade. But the marriage ended within a year.)

When Bird finally took the court for the Sycamores in the fall of 1976, he proved to be worth the wait. He led the team to a 25-3 mark while averaging 32.8 points, 13.3 rebounds, and 4.4 assists per game. That summer he won a gold medal as a member of the U.S. basketball team at the World University Games in Sophia, Bulgaria.

Bird led Indiana State to a 23-9 mark the next year and a berth in the postseason National Invitational Tournament in New York City. He made the All-American team and became eligible for the NBA draft in June because his original college class was then graduating. He still planned to play out his remaining year of eligibility, however, because he wanted a chance to win the national championship. Celtics general manager Red Auerbach selected him with Boston's first pick, believing Bird was worth waiting a year for. The move was one of the best of Auerbach's career.

The Beginning of a Rivalry

In his final season of college eligibility Bird was magnificent. Indiana State went undefeated in the regular season, with Bird averaging more than twenty-eight points and nearly fifteen rebounds a game. In the NCAA tournament the Sycamores won their first four games to advance to the championship contest against Michigan State.

The game was the first meeting between two of the greatest players to lace up a pair of sneakers. Michigan was led by its electrifying six-foot, nine-inch All-American point guard, Earvin "Magic" Johnson. Bird was virtually everyone's choice as player of the year, having led unheralded Indiana State to thirty-three consecutive victories and a number one ranking in the national polls.

The eagerly anticipated showdown was a disappointment for Bird, who was hampered by a sore thumb. He was double-teamed for most of the game and never got into the flow of the game. Johnson outscored him 24 to 19, and the Spartans won 75-64. The competition was the first of many between the two marquee players who would be credited with sparking a renewed interest in the professional game over the next decade.

The Savior

Following the NCAA tournament, Bird and the Celtics entered into serious negotiations. Boston had finished in last place in 1978–79 and was in dire need of help. Bird's agent suggested a

Bird shakes Coach Red Auerbach's hand to clinch a five-year, $3.25 million contract with the Celtics, the largest rookie contract in professional sports at the time.

salary of $1 million a year. Auerbach countered with an offer of half a million. "A cornerman can't dominate the game," he reasoned. "A big man, occasionally even a guard. But one man playing a corner can't turn a franchise around."[73] Negotiations continued, and in June, Bird signed a five-year contract for $3.25 million, at the time the largest rookie contract in the history of professional sports.

Although some observers felt Bird was too slow for the NBA, he quickly proved them wrong. He scored 14 points, with 10 rebounds and 5 assists, in his debut against the Houston Rockets. On the year, Bird averaged 21.3 points, 10.4 rebounds, and 4.5 assists per game. He was named Rookie of the Year and finished third in the Most Valuable Player voting. In addition, he was named to the All-NBA First Team for the first of eight consecutive years.

Together with Dave Cowens, Cedric Maxwell, and Nate Archibald, Bird led the Celtics to a thirty-two-game improvement over the previous season (at the time, a league record). Although the club was eventually stopped in the Eastern Conference Finals by the Philadelphia 76ers, it was clear they were headed in the right direction.

In Bird's sophomore season the Celtics added veteran center Robert Parish and rookie forward Kevin McHale to give them what would arguably become the greatest front line in the history of the league. Boston won sixty-two games during the regular season, with Bird again leading the team in scoring and rebounding. He finished second to Julius Erving in the vote for the league's Most Valuable Player.

In the playoffs the Celtics swept the Chicago Bulls to set up a rematch in the conference finals against Philadelphia. The Sixers jumped out to a three-games-to-one lead, but the Celtics bounced back to win the next two games. In the decisive seventh contest Boston completed a stunning comeback to win 91-90 on a last-minute shot by Bird.

In Game 1 of the NBA Finals the Celtics defeated the Houston Rockets by a score of 98-95. The game was decided on one of the most famous shots of Bird's career. After missing a jump shot from the right side Bird raced in to grab the rebound. In one motion he switched the ball from his right to his left hand and somehow tossed it in as he was falling out of bounds. Boston won three of the next five games, and the Celtics were NBA champions once more.

Over the next two years Bird received several individual honors. In 1981–82 he made the NBA All-Defensive Second Team for the first time and was named the Most Valuable Player of the All-Star Game. The following season he broke Sam Jones's team regular-season single-game scoring record by pouring in fifty-three points against the Indiana Pacers. In both years he was runner-up to Philadelphia's Moses Malone in the vote for the league's Most Valuable Player.

In both years, however, the Celtics came up short in their quest for another title. Despite winning a league-high sixty-three games in 1981–82, they were eliminated by the 76ers in the Eastern Conference Finals. The next season they were swept in four games by the Milwaukee Bucks in the conference semifinals. By this time Bird had solidified his standing as one of the league's great players, and over the next three seasons he raised his game to an even higher level.

Bird Versus Johnson

K.C. Jones replaced Bill Fitch as head coach of the Celtics for the 1983–84 season and guard Dennis Johnson was obtained from Phoenix. Boston proceeded to run away from the rest of the league, compiling a record of 62-20. Bird averaged more than twenty-four points per game and led the NBA in free throw percentage to win the first of three consecutive Most Valuable Player awards.

The Celtics defeated Washington in the first round of the playoffs and then knocked off the Knicks in an exciting seven-game conference semifinals series. In the Eastern Conference Finals they gained a measure of revenge by defeating the Bucks in five games. The victory set up an eagerly awaited NBA Finals series against Magic Johnson and the Los Angeles Lakers.

The two teams split the first four games, with Boston winning a pair of overtime contests. Bird scored thirty-four points in the sweltering ninety-seven-degree heat in Boston Garden in Game 5 to put the Celtics up, but the Lakers came back to even the series again in Game 6. With Bird leading the way Boston bounced back to take Game 7 to win the title. Bird was named the Most Valuable Player of the finals after averaging 27.4 points and 14 rebounds per game. He came out on top in his first postseason matchup with Johnson since the 1979 NCAA title game.

The next year Bird recorded a pair of memorable regular-season performances. In a mid-February game against the Utah Jazz, he scored thirty points with twelve rebounds, ten assists, and nine steals. Amazingly, he did this in just three quarters. With the Celtics ahead by twenty-four points, he declined to reenter the game to try for an extremely rare quadruple-double (reaching double figures in four different categories). "I already did enough damage," he said later. "Why go for it if we're up by 30?"[74]

Bird shoots a jumper over the defense of Magic Johnson of the Los Angeles Lakers. The two players shared a heated rivalry over many seasons.

Less than one month later Bird poured in sixty points in Boston's 126-115 win over the Atlanta Hawks. The mark was a new Celtics record, breaking the one set by teammate Kevin McHale just nine days earlier.

Boston won the Atlantic Division with a record of 63-19 while the Lakers took the Pacific Division at 62-20. Both clubs breezed through the first three rounds of the playoffs to meet in the finals for the second year in a row. This time Magic Johnson had his revenge as Los Angeles won in six games.

In 1985–86 the Celtics made it back to the finals once again. The Lakers, however, were upset by the Houston Rockets in the Western Conference Finals. Bird had been sensational all year. He finished the regular season fourth in scoring, seventh in rebounds, and ninth in steals. In addition, he again led the NBA in free throw percentage and finished fourth in three-point field goal percentage. He was named the league's Most Valuable Player for the third successive year, matching a record held by Bill Russell and Wilt Chamberlain.

In the NBA Finals, Houston proved to be no match for Boston. The Celtics won their sixteenth title by defeating the Rockets in six games. Bird was magnificent in the final contest, recording twenty-nine points, eleven rebounds, and twelve assists in Boston's 114-97 victory. For his efforts, he added a second NBA Finals Most Valuable Player trophy to his collection.

Bird and Johnson would meet one last time in the NBA Finals in 1986–87. Before that, however, the Celtics had to get past the Detroit Pistons in the conference finals. They did so in a seven-game series that included one of the most famous moments in playoff history.

With the series tied at two games apiece, the Pistons had a one-point lead and possession of the ball with just five seconds remaining in Game 5. As Detroit's Isiah Thomas put the ball in play, Bird streaked in to steal the pass. He fed Dennis Johnson, who scored on a layup to give the Celtics a thrilling 108-107 victory. Boston eventually won the series and moved on to face the Lakers in the NBA Finals. This time Magic Johnson dominated play, leading Los Angeles to victory in six games while winning his third NBA Finals Most Valuable Player award.

Injuries Take Their Toll

Bird was thirty years old when the 1987–88 season started. He had been bothered by back and foot problems, but his performance did not reflect them. He averaged a career-high 29.9 points per game for the year, and he became the first player in league history to hit more than half his shots from the field and 90 percent from the foul line for two seasons in a row. In the playoffs he staged a memorable duel with Dominique Wilkins in the seventh game of Boston's Eastern Conference Semifinals series with the Hawks. Wilkins outscored Bird 48-34, but twenty of Bird's points (on nine for ten shooting) came in the final period to help Boston to a 118-116 victory.

Injuries finally caught up with Bird the next season. He underwent surgery to remove bone spurs from his heels early in the year and missed all but six games. He bounced back with another solid season in 1989–90, but a herniated disc that was compressing a nerve root in his back limited him to sixty games the next year. Although surgery after the season helped ease the problem, Bird was still in pain. He played only forty-five games in 1991–92.

In the summer of 1992 Bird had one final moment of glory as a player. He was named to the Dream Team, the squad picked to represent the United States in the Summer Olympics in Barcelona, Spain. Bird helped the team to the gold medal and then returned home to announce his retirement from the game ten days later.

As head coach of the Indiana Pacers, Bird calls a play from the sidelines in a game against his former team, the Celtics.

A New Chapter

Following his retirement as an active player, Bird was hired as a special assistant to Celtics owner Paul Gaston. The position had few responsibilities, however, and when the opportunity came along to coach the Indiana Pacers in May 1997, Bird jumped at it.

Although Bird had never coached a game in his life, Pacers president Donnie Walsh thought he had the knowledge and drive necessary to be a success. "He pulls people together," says Walsh. "When he talks, you come into his world. That's what a coach has to do."[75]

Walsh's judgment proved to be correct. In his very first season in charge Bird won Coach of the Year honors as he led Indiana to fifty-eight victories. The team advanced all the way to the Eastern Conference Finals, where they were defeated by the eventual champions, the Chicago Bulls. The Pacers repeated their success the next season, this time losing in the conference finals to the New York Knicks.

In 1999–2000 Bird led Indiana to its first appearance ever in the NBA finals. The Pacers fell to the Los Angeles Lakers in six games, ending the most successful season in franchise history. That summer, however, Bird decided it was time to step down. "Three years is enough," he said. "I'm not cut out to be a coach. It's time to move on."[76]

For his accomplishments on the court, Bird was elected to the Basketball Hall of Fame in 1998. One of the greatest all-around players of all time, Bird could beat an opponent in many different ways. In addition to being a great shooter and excellent rebounder, he is probably the greatest passing forward to play the game. Together with Magic Johnson he helped spark renewed interest in the NBA at a time when the league desperately needed it. As NBA commissioner David Stern said when Bird retired, "Larry Bird has helped define the way a generation of basketball fans has come to view and appreciate the NBA."[77] It is a fitting legacy for the "Hick from French Lick."

Boston Celtics Achievements

YEAR-BY-YEAR RECORDS

Season	Coach	Finish	Regular Season		Playoffs	
			W	L	W	L
1946–47	John Russell	T5th/Eastern Div.	22	38	—	—
1947–48	John Russell	3rd/Eastern Div.	20	28	1	2
1948–49	Alvin Julian	5th/Eastern Div.	25	35	—	—
1949–50	Alvin Julian	6th/Eastern Div.	22	46	—	—
1950–51	Red Auerbach	2nd/Eastern Div.	39	30	0	2
1951–52	Red Auerbach	2nd/Eastern Div.	39	27	1	2
1952–53	Red Auerbach	3rd/Eastern Div.	46	25	3	3
1953–54	Red Auerbach	T2nd/Eastern Div.	42	30	2	4
1954–55	Red Auerbach	3rd/Eastern Div.	36	36	3	4
1955–56	Red Auerbach	2nd/Eastern Div.	39	33	1	2
1956–57	Red Auerbach	1st/Eastern Div.	44	28	7	3
1957–58	Red Auerbach	1st/Eastern Div.	49	23	6	5
1958–59	Red Auerbach	1st/Eastern Div.	52	20	8	3
1959–60	Red Auerbach	1st/Eastern Div.	59	16	8	5
1960–61	Red Auerbach	1st/Eastern Div.	57	22	8	2
1961–62	Red Auerbach	1st/Eastern Div.	60	20	8	6
1962–63	Red Auerbach	1st/Eastern Div.	58	22	8	5
1963–64	Red Auerbach	1st/Eastern Div.	59	21	8	2
1964–65	Red Auerbach	1st/Eastern Div.	62	18	8	4
1965–66	Red Auerbach	2nd/Eastern Div.	54	26	11	6
1966–67	Bill Russell	2nd/Eastern Div.	60	21	4	5
1967–68	Bill Russell	2nd/Eastern Div.	54	28	12	7
1968–69	Bill Russell	4th/Eastern Div.	48	34	12	6
1969–70	Tom Heinsohn	6th/Eastern Div.	34	48	—	—
1970–71	Tom Heinsohn	3rd/Atlantic Div.	44	38	—	—
1971–72	Tom Heinsohn	1st/Atlantic Div.	56	26	5	6
1972–73	Tom Heinsohn	1st/Atlantic Div.	68	14	7	6
1973–74	Tom Heinsohn	1st/Atlantic Div.	56	26	12	6
1974–75	Tom Heinsohn	1st/Atlantic Div.	60	22	6	5
1975–76	Tom Heinsohn	1st/Atlantic Div.	54	28	12	6
1976–77	Tom Heinsohn	2nd/Atlantic Div.	44	38	5	4

Season	Coach	Finish	Regular Season		Playoffs	
			W	L	W	L
1977–78	Tom Heinsohn 11-23					
	Tom Sanders 21-27	3rd/Atlantic Div.	32	50	—	—
1978–79	Tom Sanders 2-12					
	Dave Cowens 27-41	5th/Atlantic Div.	29	53	—	—
1979–80	Bill Fitch	1st/Atlantic Div.	61	21	5	4
1980–81	Bill Fitch	T1st/Atlantic Div.	62	20	12	5
1981–82	Bill Fitch	1st/Atlantic Div.	63	19	7	5
1982–83	Bill Fitch	2nd/Atlantic Div.	56	26	2	5
1983–84	K.C. Jones	1st/Atlantic Div.	62	20	15	8
1984–85	K.C. Jones	1st/Atlantic Div.	63	19	13	8
1985–86	K.C. Jones	1st/Atlantic Div.	67	15	15	3
1986–87	K.C. Jones	1st/Atlantic Div.	59	23	13	10
1987–88	K.C. Jones	1st/Atlantic Div.	57	25	9	8
1988–89	Jimmy Rodgers	3rd/Atlantic Div.	42	40	0	3
1989–90	Jimmy Rodgers	2nd/Atlantic Div.	52	30	2	3
1990–91	Chris Ford	1st/Atlantic Div.	56	26	5	6
1991–92	Chris Ford	T1st/Atlantic Div.	51	31	6	4
1992–93	Chris Ford	2nd/Atlantic Div.	48	34	1	3
1993–94	Chris Ford	5th/Atlantic Div.	32	50	—	—
1994–95	Chris Ford	3rd/Atlantic Div.	35	47	1	3
1995–96	M.L. Carr	5th/Atlantic Div.	33	49	—	—
1996–97	M.L. Carr	7th/Atlantic Div.	15	67	—	—
1997–98	Rick Pitino	6th/Atlantic Div.	36	46	—	—
1998–99	Rick Pitino	5th/Atlantic Div.	19	31	—	—
1999–00	Rick Pitino	5th/Atlantic Div.	35	47	—	—
2000–01	Rick Pitino 12-22					
	Jim O'Brien 24-24	5th/Atlantic Div.	36	46	—	—
Totals			2,563	1,702	272	189

Boston Celtics Awards

NBA MOST VALUABLE PLAYER
(Maurice Podoloff Trophy)

Selected by vote of NBA players until 1979–80;
by writers and broadcasters since 1980–81.

1956–57—Bob Cousy
1957–58—Bill Russell
1960–61—Bill Russell
1961–62—Bill Russell
1962–63—Bill Russell
1964–65—Bill Russell
1972–73—Dave Cowens
1983–84—Larry Bird
1984–85—Larry Bird
1985–86—Larry Bird

IBM NBA COACH OF THE YEAR
(Red Auerbach Trophy)

Selected by writers and broadcasters.
1964–65—Red Auerbach
1972–73—Tom Heinsohn
1979–80—Bill Fitch

SCHICK NBA ROOKIE OF THE YEAR
(Eddie Gottlieb Trophy)

Selected by writers and broadcasters.
1970–71—Dave Cowens, Boston
1979–80—Larry Bird

NBA EXECUTIVE OF THE YEAR

Selected by NBA executives for The Sporting News.
1979–80—Red Auerbach

NBA SIXTH MAN AWARD

Selected by writers and broadcasters.
1983–84—Kevin McHale
1984–85—Kevin McHale
1985–86—Bill Walton

NBA FINALS MOST VALUABLE PLAYER

Selected by writers and broadcasters.
1974—John Havlicek
1976—Jo Jo White
1981—Cedric Maxwell
1984—Larry Bird
1986—Larry Bird

REGULAR SEASON STATISTICAL LEADERS (YEARLY)

FIELD-GOAL PERCENTAGE

Season	Pct.	
1953–54	.486	Ed Macauley
1974–75	.539	Don Nelson
1978–79	.584	Cedric Maxwell
1979–80	.609	Cedric Maxwell
1986–87	.604	Kevin McHale
1987–88	.604	Kevin McHale

FREE-THROW PERCENTAGE

Season	Pct.	
1952–53	.850	Bill Sharman
1953–54	.844	Bill Sharman
1954–55	.897	Bill Sharman
1955–56	.867	Bill Sharman
1956–57	.905	Bill Sharman
1958–59	.932	Bill Sharman
1960–61	.921	Bill Sharman
1965–66	.881	Larry Siegfried
1968–69	.864	Larry Siegfried
1983–84	.888	Larry Bird

Season	Pct.	
1985–86	.896	Larry Bird
1986–87	.910	Larry Bird
1989–90	.930	Larry Bird

MINUTES

Season	No.	
1958–59	2,979	Bill Russell
1964–65	3,466	Bill Russell
1970–71	3,678	John Havlicek
1971–72	3,698	John Havlicek

REBOUNDING

Season	No.	
1957–58	1,564	Bill Russell
1958–59	1,612	Bill Russell
1963–64	1,930	Bill Russell
1964–65	1,878	Bill Russell

ASSISTS

Season	No.	
1952–53	547	Bob Cousy
1953–54	518	Bob Cousy
1954–55	557	Bob Cousy
1955–56	642	Bob Cousy
1956–57	478	Bob Cousy
1957–58	463	Bob Cousy
1958–59	557	Bob Cousy
1959–60	715	Bob Cousy

PERSONAL FOULS

Season	No.	
1970–71	350	Dave Cowens
1971–72	314	Dave Cowens
1975–76	356	Charlie Scott

DISQUALIFICATIONS

Season	No.	
1955–56	17	Vern Mikkelsen, Minneapolis
		Arnie Risen, Boston
1962–63	13	Frank Ramsey
1964–65	15	Tom Sanders
1965–66	19	Tom Sanders

Notes

Introduction: The Celtics Mystique

1. Quoted in Lisette Hilton, "Auerbach's Celtics Played As a Team," *SportsCentury, ESPN Classic*. www.espn.go.com.
2. Quoted in Anthony Holden, "Boston Celtics: 'The Best Known Sports Team in the World,'" *CBS Sportsline*. www.cbs.sportsline.com.

Chapter 1: The Boston Legacy

3. Quoted in Barbara Matson, "Brown a Founding Father," *Boston Globe*, November 7, 1999. www.boston.com.
4. Quoted in Peter C. Bjarkman, *Boston Celtics Encyclopedia*. Champaign, IL: Sports Publishing, 1999, p. 43.
5. Quoted in National Basketball Association, "Jim O'Brien," *NBA.Com*. www.globalnba.com.
6. Quoted in John Powers, "Banner Years," *Boston Globe*, December 23, 1999. www.boston.com.

Chapter 2: Red Auerbach

7. Quoted in Arnold "Red" Auerbach and Joe Fitzgerald, *Red Auerbach: An Autobiography*. New York: G.P. Putnam's Sons, 1977, p. 22.
8. Quoted in Kenneth Shouler, "King of the Garden," *Cigar Aficionado*. www.cigaraficionado.com.
9. Quoted in Auerbach and Fitzgerald, *Red Auerbach*, p. 30.
10. Quoted in Auerbach and Fitzgerald, *Red Auerbach*, p. 55.
11. Quoted in Auerbach and Fitzgerald, *Red Auerbach*, p. 58.
12. Quoted in Charles Moritz, ed., *Current Biography Yearbook: 1969*. New York: H.W. Wilson, 1969, p. 21.
13. Quoted in Holden, "Boston Celtics: 'The Best Known Sports

Team in the World.'"
14. Quoted in Auerbach and Fitzgerald, *Red Auerbach*, p. 135.
15. Quoted in Powers, "Banner Years."
16. Quoted in Hilton, "Auerbach's Celtics Played As a Team."
17. Quoted in Moritz, *Current Biography Yearbook: 1969*, p. 21.
18. Quoted in Hilton, "Auerbach's Celtics Played As a Team."
19. Quoted in Hilton, "Auerbach's Celtics Played As a Team."
20. Quoted in Shouler, "King of the Garden."
21. Quoted in Shouler, "King of the Garden."
22. Quoted in Shouler, "King of the Garden."
23. Quoted in National Basketball Association, "Celtics Past and Present Gather for Red Auerbach Youth Foundation," *Boston Celtics*, September 24, 2001. www.nba.com.
24. Quoted in National Basketball Association, "Celtics Name Auerbach President," *Boston Celtics*. www.nba.com.

Chapter 3: Bob Cousy

25. Quoted in Marjorie Dent Candee, ed., *Current Biography Yearbook: 1958*. New York: H.W. Wilson, 1958, p. 105.
26. Quoted in Larry Schwartz, "Celtics Tried to Pass on Ultimate Passer," *SportsCentury, ESPN*. www.espn.go.com.
27. Quoted in Bob Cousy as told to Al Hirshberg, *Basketball Is My Life*. New York: J. Lowell Pratt, 1963, p. 55.
28. Quoted in Cousy as told to Hirshberg, *Basketball Is My Life*, p. 67.
29. Quoted in Schwartz, "Celtics Tried to Pass on Ultimate Passer."
30. Quoted in Auerbach and Fitzgerald, *Red Auerbach*, p. 91.
31. Quoted in CMG Worldwide, *The Official Bob Cousy Web Site*. www.cmgww.com.
32. Quoted in Candee, *Current Biography Yearbook: 1958*, p. 106.
33. Quoted in CMG Worldwide, *The Official Bob Cousy Web Site*.
34. Quoted in Schwartz, "Celtics Tried to Pass on Ultimate Passer."
35. Quoted in Schwartz, "Celtics Tried to Pass on Ultimate Passer."

Chapter 4: Bill Russell

36. Quoted in Frank Deford, "The Ring Leader," *Sports Illustrated*, May 10, 1999, p. 102.
37. Quoted in Charles Moritz, ed., *Current Biography Yearbook: 1975*. New York: H.W. Wilson, 1975, p. 373.

38. Quoted in "The Sports 100: Bill Russell." *Sports Publishing Inc.,* Associated Press, 1999, p. 246. www.sportspublishinginc.com.

39. Quoted in Auerbach and Fitzgerald, *Red Auerbach,* p. 126.

40. Quoted in Gordon S. White Jr., "Bill Russell Named Boston Celtic Coach," *New York Times,* April 19, 1966. Reprinted in *The New York Times Encyclopedia of Sports: Basketball.* New York: Arno Press, 1979, pp. 154–55.

41. Quoted in Michael Holley, "Titles Prove He's the Won," *Boston Globe.* www.boston.com.

42. Bill Russell and Taylor Branch, *Second Wind.* New York: Random House, 1979, p. 183.

43. Quoted in Moritz, *Current Biography Yearbook: 1975,* pp. 374–375.

44. Quoted in Ron Flatter, "Russell Was Proud, Fierce Warrior," *SportsCentury, ESPN.* www.espn.go.com

Chapter 5: John Havlicek

45. Quoted in National Basketball Association, "'Havlicek Stole the Ball!'" *NBA.Com.* www.global.nba.com.

46. Quoted in Ron Fimrite, "The Valley Boys," *Sports Illustrated,* May 23, 1988, p. 84.

47. Quoted in Fimrite, "The Valley Boys," p. 84.

48. John Havlicek and Bob Ryan, *Hondo: Celtic Man in Motion.* Englewood Cliffs, NJ: Prentice-Hall, 1977, p. 48.

49. Quoted in Fimrite, "The Valley Boys," p. 85.

50. Quoted in Fimrite, "The Valley Boys," p. 85.

51. Quoted in National Basketball Association, "NBA Legends: John Havlicek."

52. Quoted in National Basketball Association, "'Havlicek Stole the Ball!'" *NBA.Com.* www.global.nba.com.

53. Quoted in National Basketball Association, "NBA Legends: John Havlicek."

54. Quoted in National Basketball Association, "NBA Legends: John Havlicek."

55. Quoted in Hillary Read, "A Legend from Start," *Boston Globe,* December 21, 1999. www.boston.com.

Chapter 6: Dave Cowens

56. Quoted in *Boston Globe,* "Cowens Played by His Own

Rules," January 13, 2002. www.boston.com.

57. Quoted in George Sullivan, *Dave Cowens: A Biography.* Garden City, NY: Doubleday, 1977, p. 15.
58. Quoted in Sullivan, *Dave Cowens*, p. 27.
59. Quoted in Sullivan, *Dave Cowens*, p. 35.
60. Quoted in Sullivan, *Dave Cowens*, p. 48.
61. Quoted in National Basketball Association, "NBA Legends: Dave Cowens," *NBA.Com.* www.global.nba.com.
62. Quoted in Sullivan, *Dave Cowens*, p. 93.
63. Quoted in National Basketball Association, "NBA Legends: Dave Cowens."
64. Quoted in Sullivan, *Dave Cowens*, p. 100.
65. Quoted in Sullivan, *Dave Cowens*, p. 122.
66. Quoted in National Basketball Association, "NBA Legends: Dave Cowens."

Chapter 7: Larry Bird

67. Quoted in National Basketball Association, "NBA Legends: Larry Bird," *NBA.Com.* www.global.nba.com.
68. Quoted in Charles Moritz, ed., *Current Biography Yearbook: 1982.* New York: H.W. Wilson, 1982, p. 34.
69. Quoted in Moritz, *Current Biography Yearbook: 1982*, p. 35.
70. Quoted in Larry Schwartz, "Plain and Simple, Bird One of the Best," *SportsCentury, ESPN.* www.espn.go.com.
71. Quoted in Frank Deford, "A Player for the Ages," *CNN/Sports Illustrated*, March 21, 1988. http://sports illustrated.cnn.com.
72. Quoted in Larry Bird with Bob Ryan, *Drive.* New York: Bantam Books, 1990, p. 15.
73. Quoted in Deford, "A Player for the Ages."
74. Quoted in "Larry Bird Timeline." *CNN/Sports Illustrated.* http://sportsillustrated.cnn.com.
75. Quoted in National Basketball Association, "NBA Legends: Larry Bird."
76. Quoted in National Basketball Association, "NBA Legends: Larry Bird."
77. Quoted in National Basketball Association, "NBA Legends: Larry Bird."

For
Further Reading

Books

Bob Cousy and Frank G. Power Jr., *Basketball Concepts and Techniques*. Boston: Allyn and Bacon, 1978. The definitive work on the techniques of playing and coaching basketball, written by one of the legends of the game.

Peter May, *The Big Three*. New York: Simon & Schuster, 1994. The story of Larry Bird, Kevin McHale, and Robert Parish, who formed what many observers consider the greatest frontcourt in the history of professional basketball.

Peter May, *The Last Banner*. Avon, MA: Adams Media, 1998. The story of the 1985-86 Boston Celtics, considered by many to be the greatest team in NBA history.

Bob Ryan and Dick Raphael, *The Boston Celtics—The History, Legends, and Images of America's Most Celebrated Team*. Reading, MA: Addison-Wesley, 1989. This coffee-table book, written by the Celtics' longest-reigning beat writer, includes season-by-season highlights of crucial games and memorable moments in the team's history.

Dan Shaughnessy, *Ever Green, the Boston Celtics—A History in the Words of Their Players, Coaches, Fans and Foes, from 1946 to the Present*. New York: St. Martin's Press, 1990. This chronological review of the team's history includes extensive observations and quotes by men who have worn the Celtic green and white.

Works Consulted

Books

Arnold "Red" Auerbach and Joe Fitzgerald, *Red Auerbach: An Autobiography*. New York: G.P. Putnam's Sons, 1977. The autobiography of the most successful coach in NBA history.

Larry Bird with Bob Ryan, *Drive*. New York: Bantam Books, 1990. The story of the Celtics all-time great who took the team from out of the cellar to three world championships.

Peter C. Bjarkman, *Boston Celtics Encyclopedia*. Champaign, IL: Sports Publishing, 1999. This comprehensive volume relates the story of professional basketball's most famous team.

Gene Brown, ed., *The New York Times Encyclopedia of Sports: Basketball*. New York: Arno Press, 1979. This volume in *The New York Times Encyclopedia of Sports* series consists of newspaper clippings detailing events in the history of basketball.

Marjorie Dent Candee, ed., *Current Biography Yearbook: 1958*. New York: H.W. Wilson, 1958. Reference volume that contains all of the biographies published in the *Current Biography* magazine in 1958.

Bob Cousy as told to Al Hirshberg, *Basketball Is My Life*. New York: J. Lowell Pratt, 1963. The heartwarming story of the rise to glory of a young man from the streets of New York to stardom in the NBA.

John Havlicek and Bob Ryan, *Hondo: Celtic Man in Motion*. Englewood Cliffs, NJ: Prentice-Hall, 1977. The autobiography of the man generally regarded as the best sixth man in NBA history.

Charles Moritz, ed., *Current Biography Yearbook: 1969*. New York: The H.W. Wilson Co., 1969. Library volume that contains all of the biographies published in the *Current Biography* magazine in 1969.

——— *Current Biography Yearbook: 1975.* New York: H.W. Wilson, 1975. Library volume that contains all of the biographies published in the *Current Biography* magazine in 1975.

——— *Current Biography Yearbook: 1982.* New York: H.W. Wilson, 1982. Library volume that contains all of the biographies published in the *Current Biography* magazine in 1982.

Bill Russell and Taylor Branch, *Second Wind.* New York: Random House, 1979. The memoirs of the Celtics' opinionated Hall of Fame center.

George Sullivan, *Dave Cowens: A Biography.* Garden City, NY: Doubleday, 1977. The biography of the Celtics' seven-time All-Star and Hall of Fame center.

Periodicals

Frank Deford, "The Ring Leader," *Sports Illustrated,* May 10, 1999, pp. 96–114.

Ron Fimrite, "The Valley Boys," *Sports Illustrated,* May 23, 1988, pp. 78–92.

Gordon S. White Jr., "Bill Russell Named Boston Celtic Coach," *New York Times,* April 19, 1966. Reprinted in *The New York Times Encyclopedia of Sports: Basketball.* New York: Arno Press, 1979, pp. 154–155.

Internet Sources *Boston Globe,* "Cowens Played by His Own Rules," January 13, 2002. www.boston.com.

CNN/Sports Illustrated, "Larry Bird Timeline." www.sportsillustrated.cnn.com.

Columbia Broadcasting System, "Alone At the Top," *CBS Sportsline.* www.cbs.sportsline.com.

Frank Deford, "A Player for the Ages," *CNN/Sports Illustrated,* March 21, 1988. http://sportsillustrated.cnn.com

Ron Flatter, "Russell Was Proud, Fierce Warrior," *SportsCentury, ESPN.* www.espn.go.com.

Lisette Hilton, "Auerbach's Celtics Played As a Team," *SportCentury, ESPN Classic.* www.espn.go.com.

Anthony Holden, "Boston Celtics: 'The Best Known Sports

Team in the World,'" *CBS Sportsline.* www.cbs.sportsline.com.

Michael Holley, "Titles Prove He's the Won," *Boston Globe,* www.boston.com.

Barbara Matson, "Brown a Founding Father," *Boston Globe,* November 7, 1999. www.boston.com.

National Basketball Association, "Celtics Name Auerbach President," *Boston Celtics.* www.nba.com.

———, "Celtics Past and Present Gather for Red Auerbach Youth Foundation," *Boston Celtics,* September 24, 2001. www.nba.com.

———, "'Havlicek Stole the Ball!'" *NBA.Com.* www.global.nba.com.

———, "Jim O'Brien," *NBA.Com.* www.nba.com.

———, "NBA Legends: Dave Cowens," *NBA.Com.* global.nba.com.

———, "NBA Legends: John Havlicek," *NBA.Com.* global.nba.com.

———, "NBA Legends: Larry Bird," *NBA.Com.* global.nba.com.

John Powers, "Banner Years," *Boston Globe,* December 23, 1999. www.boston.com.

Hillary Read, "A Legend from Start," *Boston Globe,* December 21, 1999. www.boston.com.

Larry Schwartz, "Celtics Tried to Pass on Ultimate Passer," *SportsCentury, ESPN.* www.espn.go.com.

———, "Plain and Simple, Bird One of the Best," *SportsCentury, ESPN.* www.espn.go.com.

Kenneth Shouler, "King of the Garden," *Cigar Aficionado.* www.cigaraficionado.com.

Sports Publishing Inc., "The Sports 100: Bill Russell," Associated Press, 1999. www.sportspublishinginc.com.

Websites

National Basketball Association (www.nba.com).

The Official Bob Cousy Web Site (www.cmgww.com)

Index

Picture Credits

About the Author

John F. Grabowski is a native of Brooklyn, New York. He holds a bachelor's degree in psychology from City College of New York and a master's degree in educational psychology from Teacher's College, Columbia University. He has been a teacher for thirty-one years, as well as a freelance writer specializing in the fields of sports, education, and comedy. His body of published work includes thirty-seven books; a nationally syndicated sports column; consultation on several math textbooks; articles for newspapers, magazines, and the programs of professional sports teams; and comedy material sold to Jay Leno, Joan Rivers, Yakov Smirnoff, and numerous other comics. He and his wife, Patricia, live in Staten Island with their daughter, Elizabeth.